30 Days *to* Discovering *Personal* Victory Through *Holiness*

Compiled By

Bruce Wilkinson

Multnomah®Publishers *Sisters, Oregon*

30 DAYS TO DISCOVERING PERSONAL VICTORY THROUGH HOLINESS
published by Multnomah Publishers, Inc.

© 2003 by Walk Thru the Bible
International Standard Book Number: 1-59052-070-X

Multnomah is a trademark of Multnomah Publishers, Inc.,
and is registered in the U.S. Patent and Trademark Office.
The colophon is a trademark of Multnomah Publishers, Inc.

For information:
MULTNOMAH PUBLISHERS, INC. • P.O. BOX 1720 • SISTERS, OR 97759

Library of Congress Cataloging-in-Publication Data

30 days to discovering personal victory through holiness / [compiled by Bruce Wilkinson].
    p. cm.
Includes bibliographical references.
  ISBN 1-59052-070-X (pbk.)
  1. Holiness. 2. Spiritual life—Christianity. I. Title: Thirty days to discovering personal victory
through holiness. II. Wilkinson, Bruce.

BT767 .A13 2003
248.4—dc21

2002151076

03 04 05 06 07 08—10 9 8 7 6 5 4 3 2 1 0

Read 2006

CONTENTS

SECTION 3: SEXUAL PURITY

Sexual Impurity: Countering the Devastating Epidemic

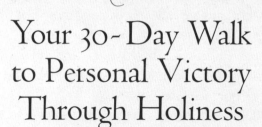

Your 30-Day Walk to Personal Victory Through Holiness

*I*f you're anything like me, sitting down to watch the evening news can be a grueling experience. Just the other day, in fact, it was reported that a five-year-old boy was gunned down in a drive-by shooting. What a tragedy!

But that's the reality of our world today: murders, drugs, bombings, rapes and other sexual crimes, domestic violence, and a myriad of similar problems.

Unfortunately, the evening news isn't the only place you hear about these things. Turn on the television during daytime or prime-time hours, and you'll get a heavy dose of these issues acted out in front of you. Hilarious sitcoms and compelling dramas have subtly taught us the wrong way to deal with relationships, manage our money, place value on things, and evaluate what is right and wrong. Even the most mundane shows often teach inappropriate ideas and behavior.

Although TV is not the only culprit in our decaying society, our culture is more and more becoming a mirror image of what it sees on the screen.

But Christians are called to become more like Christ, not like the people we see on TV. First Peter 1:15–16 commands us to be like Christ with these words: "But as He who called you is holy, you also be holy in all your conduct, because it is written, 'Be holy, for I am holy.'"

The Bible clearly instructs us in this passage, as well as in many others, that we are to be holy. First *be* holy and then *act* holy.

That's what this book is about: your personal holiness. Not when you are in heaven, or when you are ninety, but when you're in the prime of your life—like you are right at this moment.

The thirty articles you are about to read are written by godly leaders who know what it means to follow Christ. They have taken the time to learn the difference between good and evil and are following the path of personal holiness.

Some of you may be saying that it's too difficult, if not impossible, to become holy. It is true that the road is fraught with danger. Irresistible temptations stand between you and your goal of personal holiness.

But the good news is this: God doesn't expect you to do it on your own. His grace and the Holy Spirit will be right there with you, giving you the power to accomplish His will.

And with this book, you'll also have the likes of Charles Swindoll, Tony Evans, and Max Lucado to walk with you and encourage you every day of the month.

May this book be an encouragement in your pilgrimage to personal holiness.

Bruce Wilkinson

SECTION ONE

Holiness

The reason why many are still troubled,
still seeking, still making little forward
progress is because they have not yet
come to the end of themselves.

A. W. TOZER

Obedience leads to faith.
Live faithfully by the little bit of light you now have,
and you will be given more.

LOUIS CASSELS

Turning to Holiness:
The Defining Moment

By Bruce Wilkinson

If you desire Christ for a perpetual guest, give him all the keys of your heart; let not one cabinet be locked up from him; give him the range of every room and the key of every chamber.

CHARLES SPURGEON

You were nervous, that's for sure. Who wouldn't be? In just a couple of moments, you were going to walk through that door and have one of the most important interviews of your life—for the job you'd always dreamed of. Clutched in one hand was your most updated résumé (just finished late last night) and, in the other hand, a few samples of your best work.

The interview seemed to be going well until the vice president asked you to list three or four words that best described who you were as a person—outside of work. What a curveball! What would you say about yourself? Then he showed you a couple of handwritten pages and smiled, saying he had just finished calling a number of your family members and friends and had asked them the same question.

Now think for a moment: What would your closest friends say about you on a personal basis—and in only three or four words? Would any of them describe you with the word *holy*? Would you even have thought of that word? *Holy* seems like such a foreign word—more for ministers, monks, missionaries, and martyrs. Not long ago, I asked a group of men this same question, and one man said he had never dreamed he could be a "holy" man.

Obviously there are some misconceptions about what it means to be holy. Scripture says that it is the will of God that you be holy—not just your minister or "that other guy," but you.

So what does it mean to be holy? Literally, the root of the word *holy* means "to separate." For instance, if you were to cut a steak into two pieces and grill one part and save the other for another day, you would have made it "holy" in a general, nonreligious sense.

So the big idea of *holiness* includes the concept of separation. When something is separated, it is separated *from* something, as well as separated *to* something else. Take that steak again. When you cut it, you separated a piece *from* the whole, and then separated it *to* the refrigerator.

What Is God's Will?

God wants you to be a holy man. The very root, then, of His wish for you must include that you become a "separated" individual:

> "*Come out from among* them and *be separate*, says the Lord. *Do not touch what is unclean*, and I will receive you. I will be Father to you, and you shall

be My sons and daughters, says the LORD Almighty."
(2 Corinthians 6:17–18)

So, my friend, the Lord is calling you to come out and be separate and then to remain separate from that which is "unclean" and enjoy the wonderful Fatherhood of the Lord God Almighty in a depth you may never have experienced before.

PRESENT YOURSELF TO GOD TODAY

Sometimes when I disciple a man, I ask him to sketch out his entire life on a piece of paper and put in the highs and lows, the dead ends and the major achievements.

The lines always have a number of sharp turns that reflect the beginning of something entirely different in the man's life. For instance, marriage changes a man. So do children—especially that first one. A severe failure also changes a man, often plummeting him into a deep valley. The day a man meets Jesus marks him forever.

As you could imagine, each man's lifeline looks entirely different, except for one thing. Many men's lifelines have what I call a "defining moment." Men describe it differently, but they all basically say the same thing. See if you can identify with this man's rambling words:

> You know, after I became a Christian, I grew for a while but then, uh, well, I just kind of, uh, strayed away, you know, from the Lord. Years went by when I kind of, you know, left the church, or just rebelled against what I knew God wanted. But then right there (he points to a major upturn on his lifeline), I rededicated my life to God. That was a true turnaround for

me. Not that I'm perfect, but I really started growing after I did that. That's when I really sold out to God and stopped playing church and started serving God with my whole heart.

Sound familiar?

COUNT THE COST

Jesus knew that the secret to a man's ultimate victory in his spiritual life has a lot to do with that "defining moment." In fact, Jesus said that if a man does not choose Christ above everyone and everything, then that man would not become a full-grown disciple of His. Jesus said that not only would that man never become a disciple if he didn't make a decision for Christ, but that he actually *could not!*

You see, after you are saved you must face the Lord's call on your heart. He doesn't seek part of it or most of it; rather, Christ seeks to be the very Master of your heart. If you don't choose to present yourself, you'll never become a truly holy man.

Holiness always starts with the heart. Holiness starts not with the externals, but with the internals. Not with a set of rules and regulations, but with a relationship of trust and complete dedication. Read the words of Jesus about what He's calling you to do: "If anyone desires to come after Me, let him deny himself, and take up his cross, and follow Me" (Matthew 16:24).

Challenging words, right from the lips of the Lord. Do you see what Jesus says must be true of those who desire to come after Him? You must deny yourself and take up your cross and then follow Him. The first key to pursuing holiness is found in those very first words: "If anyone desires to come after Me." Why? Because without a desire to come after Jesus, you will never pay the price He asks.

It's Up to You

Now, let me ask you a rather sobering question: Have you made a decision to pursue personal holiness? No matter how unholy you may have been, or how unholy you may be at this present moment, you can make today a day of new beginnings. A new start. A putting off the old and putting on the new. Perhaps the best way to launch such a new beginning with the Lord is to pray and tell Him about your honest desire to become a holy man and then ask Him to enable you by His grace and His Holy Spirit.

> If for one whole day, quietly and determinedly, we were to give ourselves up to the ownership of Jesus and to obeying His orders, we should be amazed at its close to realize all He had packed into that one day. (Oswald Chambers)

On October 4, 1997, over one million men gathered in Washington, D.C., to do just that. It was the Promise Keepers "Stand in the Gap" rally, and men came from all over the country to be part of it. At one point during the rally, these hundreds of thousands of men all knelt down and prayed silently for forgiveness for their sins. The scene was awesome! Over one million men on their faces before God! It was so quiet I could hear the birds chirping. For many of those men, that rally was a "defining moment."

But you don't have to go anywhere to have a defining moment. You can do it right where you're sitting. If you've never experienced a defining moment, I pray that today will be that day. The selections you are about to read will help you discover what it means to deny yourself, take up your cross, and follow Christ. These are the important keys to opening the doors of holiness.

If you have already experienced a defining moment, praise God! You've already begun the magnificent journey of discipleship and are growing in Christ. I think you'll find that the following articles will confirm your direction and encourage you to continue the pursuit of personal holiness.

Either way, God's will for your life is that you *be holy* and *act holy.* Are you ready to submit to His will?

Chapter 1

Holiness

By John White

The destined end of man is not happiness, nor health, but holiness.
God's one aim is the production of saints. He is not an eternal blessing
machine for men; he did not come to save men out of pity;
he came to save men because he had created them to be holy.

Oswald Chambers

Have you ever gone fishing in a polluted river and hauled out an old shoe, a teakettle, or a rusty can? I get a similar sort of catch if I cast as a bait the word *holiness* into the murky depths of my mind. To my dismay, I come up with such associations as:

- thinness
- hollow-eyed gauntness
- beards
- sandals
- long robes
- stone cells
- no sex
- no jokes

- hair shirts
- frequent cold baths
- fasting
- hours of prayer
- wild, rocky deserts
- getting up at 4 A.M.
- clean fingernails
- stained glass
- self-humiliation

The list is a strange one. Some items suggest you can only achieve holiness by a painful and rigorous process. Yet many teachers claim that your most intense efforts will be vain since holiness is something God gives, not something you achieve. Again, my juxtaposition of items lends an air of frivolity to a subject which none of us dare take lightly. If the means by which men and women have sought holiness seem ridiculous, we should weep rather than laugh.

More important, my mental flotsam and jetsam point to something unreal in our views of holiness. Take the items "robes, sandals, beards." We picture Jesus so. Hence, while consciously aware that His robes and beard have little to do with His holiness, we unconsciously lump them all together. If you doubt what I say, try to picture Jesus with a mustache, wearing blue jeans, and riding a bicycle. If you are anything like most of us, you will be shocked even though you are aware intellectually that there is nothing unholy about jeans or bikes, and no moral reason why Jesus would not in the twentieth century make use of either of them.

Our paradoxical reactions are a clue to artificiality in our thinking about holiness and about God's Holy One. For while in one sense holiness has to do with the "wholly other," it yet must penetrate to the most mundane of our daily activities so that the division between sacred and secular vanishes entirely from our lives.

THE GOD WHO IS HOLY

Two ideas are paramount when the Bible talks about God's holiness—an attribute which more than any other seems to express the essence of what God is. One idea has to do with separateness and difference. God is wholly unlike anything we can conceive or know. He is infinitely greater and more powerful, besides being qualitatively, utterly dissimilar from us and from the universe He created. Though we are made in His image, and therefore reflect His being, the difference is such as to create a chasm of endless depth between what He is and what we are. "I am what I am," says God, "and there is nothing with which I can be compared."

The second idea has to do with morality. Bound up in the qualitative difference I have mentioned is ultimate ethical beauty and moral perfection. God's holiness is not merely total separation from uncleanness, but a positive goodness beyond our capacity to conceive. The very heavens are unclean in His sight. Yet it is this same goodness and beauty which He wants to share with you. He wants you to be like Him.

You will never understand Him, yet you are called to know Him. You are different from Him, yet He wants to give you the quality which most distinguishes Him from you. You are redeemed to be set aside for God's special use and made a partaker of His moral perfection.

THE VERDICT

When you became a Christian, God did much more than forgive your sins. He made you righteous. He, the judge of dead and living, pronounced you "not guilty"! He now looks upon you and behaves toward you as though you were perfectly righteous. He does not deceive Himself about you. Rather, your hand is held by the hand of the Christ who redeemed you by His blood.

The process by which you were pronounced righteous and by which your peace was made with God is called justification. "Therefore, since we are justified by faith, we have peace with God through our Lord Jesus Christ" (Romans 5:1, RSV).

But God did more than justify you. He sanctified you. Not content with declaring you righteous, He began to share His holiness with you.

You may not have noticed my definition of *sanctification* a page or so back. God did two things when He sanctified you. By an operation of the Holy Spirit, He set you apart for His own exclusive use. In addition, He began a process within you to fit you for divine use. He began by the Holy Spirit to make you a holy person.

What you did not anticipate after so auspicious a beginning was the intense struggle and the dismal failure that came later. You failed to grasp the nature of the struggle, not realizing that neither the Holy Spirit nor your sinful tendencies would ever reach a compromise.

You were justified and you were sanctified. The question is, What went wrong with the sanctifying process? How may it be reestablished?

THE TRANSFORMATION PROCESS

"Do not be conformed to this world but be transformed" (Romans 12:2, RSV).

Transformation is not an overnight matter. It takes a lifetime, but continuous progress in holiness is assured.

Therefore, beware of any book or teaching which purports to teach "one simple secret" of "victory" or of sanctification. There is nothing secret about the process. The book may indeed have something helpful to offer. But nothing—no faith, no yielding, no "letting go and letting God"—can begin the sanctifying process within you. And no secret can complete the process overnight. If you are a Christian, the process has already begun. So far as God is concerned, you are already "set apart" for His sacred service. And the Holy Spirit is eager for the process of fitting you to continue.

God's Works or Yours?

A paragraph back I referred to the phrase "let go and let God." This was a catch phrase of obscure origins from the late nineteenth century. A college student is alleged to have written on six postcards the letters *LETGOD* and placed the six cards on the mantelpiece of his room. As a draught blew down the letter *D,* he is said to have discovered the secret of letting God control his life by letting go of it himself.

Many people have found the words helpful. Nevertheless, they raise a serious issue about holiness over which Christians disagree. Some see holiness as a work of God to which the Christian makes no contribution. My part as a Christian is simply to relinquish control. His part is to work through me. My efforts to strive after holiness will be unavailing. In me—that is, in my flesh—dwells no good thing so that I have nothing of value to contribute. I therefore trust—that is, I rest in His goodness. I do not struggle to control my temper, but allow Christ to handle my angry feelings. I say with Paul, "Not I, but Christ." It is as though, like a sea captain, I have been up to this point at the helm of my life, and now Another is going to take over. Even faith is seen as a passivity of the will—a resting and a relaxing, not a seizing or appropriating.

THE TWO VIEWS OF HOLINESS

I want to call this view the passive view of holiness in contrast with what might be called the active view, by which the Christian is called on to "wrestle and fight and pray."

Teachers of the active schools stress what they call "the means of grace." Yielding may be good, but must not exclude watching and prayer, meditation on the Scriptures, fellowship with other believers, a careful effort to "maintain good works," a deliberate attempt to refrain from sin and to perform active Christian duties.

You will be puzzled as you talk to exponents of both schools to find they can give convincing and sincere testimonies to the blessings they have received as a result of practicing what seem to be conflicting principles. All schools are agreed that faith is the key issue. All schools are agreed that human efforts alone are unavailing and that the power for holy living must come from God. All schools are agreed that the basis of sanctification is God's intervention in the incarnation, death, resurrection, and ascension of His Son, Jesus Christ, and that the help is mediated by the Holy Spirit, who brings about the believer's union with Christ. But given the general points of agreement, the words and phrases used become confusing and contradictory.

It need not surprise us that there should be confusion and difficulty. In the first place, the New Testament itself seems to express both points of view. "Work out your own salvation with fear and trembling," writes Paul to the Philippians, apparently espousing an active view of the

Christian life. Yet, with no pause, he goes on: "for [because] God is at work in you, both to will and to work for his good pleasure" (Philippians 2:12–13, RSV). Now if you had only the words in the second part of the sentence, you might conclude that a Christian should be passive in the hands of a God who actively worked within him. And notice, God not only makes a man do what God wants, but God also actually makes the decision inside him—that is, causes him to will.

Yet to Paul there seems to be no conflict between the first part of the sentence and the second. We are to work because God is working in us. The New Testament consistently presents both what I have called the passive and the active approaches to holiness without any sense of contradiction.

It may be well for us to realize that we are dealing with one of the great mysteries in Scripture: the mystery of the interaction between your will and God's. The glorious work of delivering you from sin, making something altogether wonderful out of you, is a work in which both you and God have a part. Trouble arises when you start trying to map out where God's part stops and your part begins.

Let there be no misunderstanding. Without God's Spirit within, our efforts are futile. No good thing could spring from our corrupt and sinful hearts. But we have been redeemed and we have been sanctified. We have been set apart for God's use. Let us then agree with God in the matter. If yielding means bowing down to Him as King, let us day by day, hour by hour yield every part of our beings in allegiance to Him. Let us reserve no part of our lives to serve selfish interests and ambitions. But having done that, let us assume the whole armor of God and by miraculous strength declare war on all that is evil within and without.

STUDY QUESTIONS

1. When you think about God, what is the first thing that usually comes to mind? Do your thoughts about Him line up with His holiness as depicted in Scripture? Or are they more in line with what you think He should be?

2. Because God has set you apart for His own exclusive use, have you submitted to His will in your day-to-day life? Take some time to pray and ask God how you can get involved in what He is doing in your life, the lives of those around you, and in the world. What does Scripture say you should be doing?

Taken from *The Fight* by John White. Copyright © 1976 InterVarsity Christian Fellowship/USA. Used by permission of InterVarsity Press, P.O. Box 1400, Downers Grove, IL 60515. www.ivpress.com.

Chapter 2

What Holiness Is, and Why It Matters

By J. I. Packer

Just as he who called you is holy, so be holy in all you do;
for it is written: "Be holy, because I am holy."

1 PETER 1:15–16, NIV

Make every effort...to be holy; without holiness no one will see the Lord.

HEBREWS 12:14, NIV

Our grandfather clock, which tells us not only the hours, minutes, and seconds, but also the days of the week, the months of the year, and the phases of the moon, is something of a veteran. Scratched on one of its lead weights is the date 1780—the year of the French Revolution and George Washington's first term as president.

It is a musical clock, too, of a rather unusual sort. Not only does it strike the hour, but it also has a built-in carillon (knobs on a brass cylinder tripping hammers that hit bells, which play a tune for three minutes every three hours). Two of its four tunes we recognize, for we hear them still today. However, the other two, which sound like country dances, are unknown—not just to us but to everyone who has heard them played. Over the years they were forgotten, which is a pity, for they are good tunes, and we would like to know something about them.

In the same way, the historic Christian teaching on holiness has been largely forgotten, and that also is a pity, for it is central to the glory of God and the good of souls.

OUR CHRISTIAN HERITAGE OF HOLINESS

There was a time when all Christians laid great emphasis on the reality of God's call to holiness and spoke with deep insight about His enabling of us for it. Evangelical Protestants, in particular, offered endless variations on the themes of what God's holiness requires of us, what our holiness involves for us, by what means and through what disciplines the Holy Spirit sanctifies us, and the ways in which holiness increases our assurance and joy and usefulness to God.

The Puritans insisted that all life and relationships must become "holiness to the Lord." John Wesley told the world that God had raised up Methodism "to spread scriptural holiness throughout the land." Phoebe Palmer, Handley Moule, Andrew Murray, Jessie Penn-Lewis, F. B. Meyer, Oswald Chambers, Horatius Bonar, Amy Carmichael, and L. B. Maxwell are only a few of the leading figures in the "holiness revival" that touched all evangelical Christendom between the mid-nineteenth and mid-twentieth centuries.

But how different it is today! To listen to our sermons and to read the books we write for each other, and then to watch the zany, worldly, quarrelsome way we behave as Christian people, you would never imagine that once the highway of holiness was clearly marked out for Bible-believers, so that ministers and people knew what it was and could speak of it with authority and confidence.

DEFINING HOLINESS

But what exactly is holiness?

Consider first the word itself. *Holiness* is a noun that belongs with the adjective *holy* and the verb *sanctify,* which means "to make holy." (It is a pity in one way that we have to draw on two word groups in English to cover what is a single word group in both Hebrew and Greek, but the verb *holify* would be so ugly that maybe we should be glad it does not exist.)

Holy in both biblical languages means "separated and set apart for God, consecrated and made over to Him." In its application to people, God's "holy ones" or "saints," the word implies both devotion and assimilation: devotion, in the sense of living a life of service to God; assimilation, in the sense of imitating, conforming to, and becoming like the God one serves.

HOLINESS HAS TO DO WITH MY HEART

Holiness starts inside a person, with a right purpose that seeks to express itself in a right performance. It is a matter not just of the motions that I go through, but of the motives that prompt me to go through them.

A holy person's motivating aim, passion, desire, longing, aspiration, goal, and drive is to please God, both by what one does and by what one avoids doing. In other words, one practices good works and cuts out evil ones. Good works begin with praise, worship, and honoring and exalting of God as the temper of one's whole waking life. Evil works start with neglect of these things, and coolness with regard to them. So I must labor to keep my heart actively responsive to God.

But asceticism, as such—voluntary abstinence, routines of self-deprivation and grueling austerity—is not the same thing as holiness, though some forms of asceticism may well find a place in a holy person's life.

Nor is formalism, in the sense of outward conformity in word and deed to the standards God has set, anything like holiness, though assuredly there is no holiness without such conformity.

Nor is legalism, in the sense of doing things to earn God's favor or to earn more of it than one has already, to be regarded as holiness. Holiness is always the saved sinner's response of gratitude for grace received.

The Pharisees of Jesus' day made all three mistakes, yet were thought to be very holy people until Jesus told them the truth about themselves and the inadequacies of their supposed piety. After that, however, we dare not forget that holiness begins in the heart. Who wants to line up with those Pharisees?

IS HOLINESS IMPORTANT TODAY?

But is holiness really important? Does it matter, in the final analysis, whether Christ's professed followers live holy lives or not?

From watching today's Christian world (and in particular the great evangelical constituency of North America), you might easily conclude that it does not matter. I once had to respond in print to the question, "Is personal holiness passé?" I found it hard not to conclude that most present-day believers deep down think it is passé. Here is some of the evidence for that conclusion.

Preaching and Teaching

What do we Christians mainly preach and teach and produce TV programs and videocassettes about these days? The answer seems to be not holiness, but success and positive feelings: getting health, wealth, freedom from care, good sex, and happy families. I remember seeing in a Christian journal a group of eight new "how-to" books reviewed on a single page. How long, I wonder, is it since you heard about eight new books on holiness? Shall I guess?

Leadership

What do we Christians chiefly value in our leaders—our preachers, teachers, pastors, writers, televangelists, top people in parachurch ministries, moneymen who bankroll churches and other Christian enterprises, and other folk with key roles in our setup?

The answer seems to be not their holiness, but their gifts and skills and resources. The number of North American leaders (and other Christians too) who in recent years have been found guilty of sexual and financial shenanigans, and who when challenged have declined to see themselves as accountable to any part of the body of Christ, is startling.

Much more startling is the way in which, after public exposure and some few slaps on the wrist, they are soon able to resume their ministry and carry on as if nothing had happened, commanding apparently as much support as before. To protest that Christians believe in the forgiveness of sins and the restoration of sinners is beside the point. What I am saying is that the speed of their reinstatement shows that we value them more for their proven gifts than for their proven sanctity, since the thought that only holy people are likely to be spiritually useful does not loom large in our minds.

Evangelism

How do we Christians formulate the gospel to others in our evangelism, and to ourselves as born-again believers who are called to live by it? I do not think it can be disputed that while we lay heavy stress on faith (coming to Christ, trusting His promises, believing that God knows what He is doing with our lives, and hoping for heaven), we touch very lightly on repentance (binding one's conscience to God's moral law, confessing and forsaking one's sins, making restitution for past wrongs, grieving before God at the dishonor one's sins have done Him, and forming a game plan for holy living).

The post-Christian culture of the West doubts whether there are any moral absolutes. It is sure that, in any case, private morality or immorality really matters to nobody except the persons directly involved. Western Christians act as if they agreed, especially where sex and shekels (H. Hensley Henson's apt phrase) are concerned.

Some Christians even argue that to speak of repentance as a necessity rather than a mere beneficial option, and to affirm that the gospel call to faith is also a call to repentance, is to lapse into anti-Christian legalism. You have heard, I am sure, many, many sermons on faith. How often, I wonder, have you heard a series, or even one sermon, preached on repentance? You have books in your home on living the Christian life successfully. Do they even mention repentance, let alone make much of it as a vital, lifelong discipline?

When you explain the gospel to others, do you emphasize repentance, and the holiness by which repentance is expressed, as a spiritual necessity? Shall I guess?

But if we play down or ignore the importance of holiness, we are utterly and absolutely wrong.

Holiness is, in fact, commanded. God wills it, Christ requires it, and all the Scriptures—the Law, the Gospels, the prophets, the wisdom writings, the Epistles, the history books that tell of judgments past, and the book of Revelation that tells of judgment to come—call for it.

> In reality, holiness is the goal of our redemption. As Christ died in order that we may be justified, so we are justified in order that we may be sanctified and made holy. Holiness is the object of our new creation. We are born again so that we may grow up into Christlikeness.

Holiness is actually the true health of the person. Anything else is ugliness and deformity at character level, a malfunctioning of the individual, a crippled state of soul. The various forms of bodily sickness and impairment that Jesus healed are so many illustrations of this deeper inward deformity.

Holiness effectively thwarts Satan in his designs on our lives. By contrast, unconcern about holiness and failure to practice the purity and righteousness to which we are called play into his hands every time.

) Righteousness, meaning holy integrity and uprightness, is the breastplate in the armor of God that Christians are called to wear in order to counter the devil's attacks (Ephesians 6:14).

Holiness also gives credibility to witness. But those who proclaim a life-changing Savior will not impress others if their own lives seem to be no different from anyone else's. Holy ways will enhance our testimony, while worldly ways will undermine it. "You are the light of the world.... Let your light shine before men, that they may see your good deeds [good works, backing up good words] and praise your Father in heaven [about whom you told them, and whose power they now see in your living]" (Matthew 5:14, 16, NIV).

If we want to be fruitful in evangelism, we must cultivate holiness of life.

√Finally, holiness is the substance of which happiness is

the spin-off. Those who chase happiness miss it, while to those who pursue holiness through the grace of Christ, happiness of spirit comes unasked. "I delight in your commands because I love them.... They are the joy of my heart" (Psalm 119:47, 111, NIV).

Can anyone still doubt, after all this, that for every Christian, without exception, holiness is important?

STUDY QUESTIONS

1. Is personal holiness an action, an attitude, or both? Explain your answer.

2. Why is it that the topic of holiness is so seldom taught today? Has this lack of instruction had an effect on your life? How?

3. Do you think holiness is a primary concern in your church? What can you do to help your church place more emphasis on practical holiness?

From *Rediscovering Holiness*, by J. I. Packer. © 1992, 1999 by J. I. Packer. Published by Servant Publications, P.O. Box 8617, Ann Arbor, Michigan, 48107. Used with permission.

Chapter 3

Abiding in Christ:
The Source of Holiness

BY NEIL ANDERSON AND ROBERT SAUCY

"Abide in Me, and I in you. As the branch cannot bear fruit of itself,
unless it abides in the vine, so neither can you, unless you abide in Me.
I am the vine, you are the branches; he who abides in Me and I in him,
he bears much fruit; for apart from Me you can do nothing."

JOHN 15:4–5, NASB

While speaking to adult Christian groups in evangelical churches several years ago, I (Neil) would make the following statement: "Christian maturity is understanding the principles of the Bible and trying as best we can to live them." I then asked how many people agreed with that statement. Nearly everybody did.

Then I told them I disagreed with almost every aspect of that statement! It's true that understanding the principles of Scripture is essential for Christian maturity, but that in itself is not Christian maturity.

Christian maturity is Christlike character. If you know all the principles but don't have the character, then you are only a "resounding gong or a clanging cymbal" that is without love

(1 Corinthians 13:1, NIV). Also, trying as best you can to live the Christian life will probably bear no fruit because apart from Christ you can do nothing. Only by God's grace can you live the Christian life.

Progressive sanctification is a supernatural work. Clearly, the victory over sin and death through Christ's crucifixion and resurrection was God's victory and not ours. Only God can redeem us from the power of sin, set us free from our past, and make us new creations "in Christ." Even though we have become partakers of the divine nature due to Christ's presence in our lives, we still need to be dependent upon God to supply the power to conform us to His image.

Becoming a Christian does not mean that we have more power in and of ourselves. It means that we are inwardly connected to the only source of power that is able to overcome the laws of sin and death, which is the law of the Spirit of life in Christ Jesus (Romans 8:2).

That we are tempted to misunderstand this truth or perhaps unconsciously forget it in our attempt to grow as believers is seen in Paul's sharp question to the Galatians: "Are you so foolish? After beginning with the Spirit, are you now trying to attain your goal by human effort?" (Galatians 3:3, NIV).

ABIDING IN CHRIST

Progress in the Christian life is attained through living in union with Christ through faith. This thought is expressed in a variety of ways:

- "As you therefore have received Christ Jesus the Lord, so walk in Him, having been firmly rooted and now being built up in Him and established in your faith, just as you were instructed" (Colossians 2:6–7, NASB).

- "I no longer live, but Christ lives in me. The life I live in the body, I live by faith in the Son of God" (Galatians 2:20, NIV).
- "Be strong in the Lord and in his mighty power" (Ephesians 6:10, NIV).
- We grow by "holding fast to the head," which is Christ (Colossians 2:19, NASB).
- "Clothe yourselves with the Lord Jesus Christ, and do not think about how to gratify the desires of the sinful nature" (Romans 13:14, NIV).
- "Whatever you do, whether in word or deed, do it all in the name of the Lord Jesus" (Colossians 3:17, NIV). (See 1 Peter 3:16—our behavior is to be in Christ.)

It is clear from these verses that our life, strength, and all our activities as believers are to be related to Christ. They are to flow out of our being in union with Christ. This truth could not be made clearer than it is in Jesus' statement about the necessity of abiding in Him: "Abide in Me, and I in you. As the branch cannot bear fruit of itself, unless it abides in the vine, so neither can you, unless you abide in Me.... For apart from Me you can do nothing" (John 15:4–5, NASB).

The Greek word translated *abide* also means *remain*, or *continue*. But in the Gospel of John, in the context of a relationship with Christ, it denotes more than a static relationship. Paul's statements about being "in Christ" and having "Christ in us" are expanded upon in John's concept of "abiding in," which expresses a dynamic, intimate union with that person.

What this all-embracing concept means in our relationship to Christ is seen in the relationship between the Father and Christ. Even as we abide in Christ and He in us, so do the Son and the Father abide in each other. The result of Christ abiding in His Father is that everything He says and does manifests the character of the Father.

We have the same kind of relationship with Christ that Christ has with the Father. We abide in Christ, and Christ abides in us. Through this mutual abiding, Christ conveys His life to us so that our lives display His character as we trust and obey Him.

THE PRACTICE OF ABIDING IN CHRIST

Scripture reveals that abiding in Christ involves two basic practices: First, it means that we nourish ourselves through faith in all that Christ is to us; and second, it means that we follow Him in obedience to His commands. In a very real sense we are back to the simple concepts of trust and obey.

Receiving Christ by Faith

Abiding in Christ means first to receive His life and saving work into our own life through faith. In a vivid statement depicting appropriation and assimilation, Jesus said, "He who eats My flesh and drinks My blood abides in Me, and I in him" (John 6:56, NASB). Jesus is not talking about literal eating and drinking, but as is clear from an earlier statement, He is talking about receiving Him and His work through faith. In this context, eating is synonymous with believing: "I am the bread of life; he who comes to Me shall not hunger, and he who believes in Me shall never thirst" (John 6:35, NASB). In the spiritual life, hunger and thirst are satisfied by coming to Christ or believing in Him.

Abiding in Christ, then, means first to receive by faith all that Christ is for us. In Him we are rightly related to God as His beloved children. We are alive with His victorious eternal life. We are, in Paul's words, "blessed...with every spiritual blessing in the heavenly places in Christ" (Ephesians 1:3, NASB).

Obeying God's Commands

When Jesus said He abided in His Father, He was saying that He lived in total obedience to Him. Likewise, for us to abide in Christ means that we live in obedience to our Lord's commands. This second aspect of abiding in Christ was suggested by Jesus Himself when He said that His words were to abide in us (John 15:7). They are to so lodge in our minds and hearts that they will naturally direct our actions in a life of conformity to Christ. In the illustration of the vine and the branches (John 15:1–8), this is represented by the fruit that inevitably results when a person is abiding in the vine.

Christ makes it clear that obedience is an aspect of abiding when He says, "Abide in My love; just as I have kept My Father's commandments, and abide in His love" (John 15:10, NASB). Keeping Jesus' commands includes walking after His pattern of life. This means showing the same kind of love He showed. Jesus said, "A new commandment I give to you, that you love one another, even as I have loved you" (John 13:34, NASB).

We are to look to Jesus' example as a pattern for our own lives: "A pupil [or disciple] is not above his teacher" (Luke 6:40, NASB). First John 2:6 adds, "The one who says he abides in Him ought himself to walk in the same manner as He walked" (NASB).

Living in union with Christ, which is essential for growth in holiness, involves both our constant receiving of supernatural life from the vine and a determination to follow Christ in our daily walk. Jesus' illustration of the vine and the branches makes this absolutely clear. Reading this passage about fruit-bearing, we subtly hear and focus on an imperative to bear fruit. Elsewhere in Scripture, we see this fruit described in terms of our moral and ethical behavior.

But before we can bear fruit, Jesus tells us first to "abide in Me...abide in My love" (John 15:4, 9, NASB). Just as a branch bears fruit by abiding in the vine, so we are able to live out Scripture's commands by nourishing ourselves on Christ's life. As one scholar explains, the loyalty demanded in abiding in Christ is "not primarily a continued being for, but a being from; it is not the holding of a position, but an allowing oneself to be held." The relationship is reciprocal, but the action of the branch is totally dependent on the life from the vine.

THE PRIORITY IN ABIDING IN CHRIST

That our nourishment from Christ precedes our ability to obey is seen in Jesus' command to love one another (John 15:12, 17). But we cannot show this love unless we are abiding in God's love (v. 9) or continuing in the love that we have received: "We love because he first loved us" (1 John 4:19, NIV). It is futile to attempt to love other people unless we first nourish ourselves daily by receiving afresh God's love for us. Only as we receive God's love for us and respond in love can we obey His commandments. Our obedience is possible only as a result of the love we have for Christ: "If you love me, you will obey what I command" (John 14:15, NIV; see also verse 21).

Conforming to the image of God is a long and steady process of internal change as we abide in Christ. People simply do not change overnight, nor can they be forced to do so. Abiding in Christ is being yoked to the gentle Jesus (Matthew 11:29). Servants of Christ who minister to others know that and, like Christ, show great patience and gentleness.

STUDY QUESTIONS

1. The most important part of your strategy to achieve personal victory through holiness is to become a follower of Jesus Christ. If you have not done this, take a moment right now to confess your sins to Christ, ask for His forgiveness, and give your entire life to Him. The cost to be a follower of Christ is your life, but the rewards are eternal.

2. If you are a follower of Christ, the next step is to abide in Him. That means obedience to His commands. Take a moment to list a few of His commands that immediately come to mind.

3. Do you know what Christ's greatest command is? The second greatest?

Taken from *The Common Made Holy*, by Neil Anderson and Robert Saucy. Copyright © 1997 by Harvest House Publishers, Eugene, OR. Used by permission.

Chapter 4

Holiness Is for You

By Jerry Bridges

For sin shall not be your master,
because you are not under law, but under grace.

Romans 6:14, NIV

The shrill ring of the telephone shattered the stillness of the beautiful, crisp Colorado morning. On the other end was one of those utterly impossible individuals God seems to have sprinkled around here on earth to test the grace and patience of His children.

He was in top form that morning—arrogant, impatient, demanding. I hung up the phone seething inside with anger, resentment, and perhaps even hatred. Grabbing my jacket, I walked out into the cold air to try to regain my composure. The quietness of my soul, so carefully cultivated in my "quiet time" with God that morning, had been ripped into shreds and replaced with a volatile, steaming emotional volcano.

As my emotions subsided, my anger turned to utter discouragement. It was only 8:30 in the morning and my day was ruined. Not only was I discouraged; I was confused. Only two hours before, I had read Paul's emphatic declaration, "For sin shall not be your master, because you are not under law, but under grace." But despite this nice-sounding promise of victory over sin, there I was locked in the viselike grip of anger and resentment.

"Does the Bible really have any answers for real life?" I asked myself that morning. With all my heart, I desired to live an obedient, holy life; yet there I was utterly defeated by one phone call.

Perhaps this incident has a familiar ring to you. The circumstances probably differed, but your reaction was similar. Perhaps your problem is anger with your children, or a temper at work, or an immoral habit you can't overcome, or maybe several "besetting sins" that dog you day in and day out.

THERE ARE ANSWERS

Whatever your particular sin problem (or problems), the Bible does have the answer for you. There is hope. You and I can walk in obedience to God's Word and live a life of holiness. In fact, God expects every Christian to live a holy life. But holiness is not only expected; it is the promised birthright of every Christian. Paul's statement is true. Sin shall not be our master.

The concept of holiness may seem a bit archaic to our current generation. To some minds, the very word *holiness* brings images of bunned hair, long skirts, and black stockings. To others, the idea is associated with a repugnant holier-than-thou attitude. Yet holiness is very much a scriptural idea. The word *holy* in various forms occurs more than six hundred times in the Bible. One entire book, Leviticus, is devoted to the subject, and the idea of holiness is woven elsewhere throughout the fabric of Scripture. More importantly, God specifically commands us to be holy (Leviticus 11:44).

The Myths of Holiness

The idea of exactly how to be holy has suffered from many false concepts. In some circles, holiness is equated with a series of specific prohibitions—usually in such areas as smoking, drinking, and dancing. The list of prohibitions varies depending on the group. When we follow this approach to holiness, we are in danger of becoming like the Pharisees with their endless lists of trivial dos and don'ts, and their self-righteous attitude. For others, holiness means a particular style of dress and mannerisms. And for still others, it means unattainable perfection—an idea that fosters either delusion or discouragement about one's sin.

All of these ideas, while accurate to some degree, miss the true concept. To be holy is to be morally blameless. It is to be separated from sin and, therefore, consecrated to God. The word signifies "separation to God, and the conduct befitting those so separated."

Perhaps the best way of understanding the concept of holiness is to note how writers of the New Testament used the word. In 1 Thessalonians 4:3–7, Paul used the term in contrast to a life of immorality and impurity. Peter used it in contrast to living according to the evil desires we had when we lived outside of Christ (1 Peter 1:14–16). John contrasted one who is holy with those who do wrong and are vile (Revelation 22:11). To live a holy life, then, is to live a life in conformity to the moral precepts of the Bible and in contrast to the sinful ways of the world. It is to live a life characterized by "[putting] off your old self, which is being corrupted by its deceitful desires…and [putting] on the new self, created to be like God in true righteousness and holiness" (Ephesians 4:22, 24, NIV).

WHERE HAS IT GONE?

If holiness, then, is so basic to the Christian life, why do we not experience it more in daily living? Why do so many Christians feel constantly defeated in their struggle with sin?

Why does the church of Jesus Christ so often seem to be more conformed to the world around it than to God?

At the risk of oversimplification, the answers to these questions can be grouped into three basic problem areas.

Our first problem is that our attitude toward sin is more self-centered than God-centered. We are more concerned about our own "victory" over sin than we are about the fact that our sins grieve the heart of God. We cannot tolerate failure in our struggle with sin chiefly because we are success-oriented, not because we know it is offensive to God.

W. S. Plummer said, "We never see sin aright until we see it as against God…. All sin is against God in this sense: that it is His law that is broken, His authority that is despised, His government that is set at naught…. Pharaoh and Balaam, Saul and Judas each said, 'I have sinned against heaven and before thee' and David said, 'Against Thee, Thee only have I sinned.'"

God wants us to walk in obedience, not in victory. Obedience is oriented toward God; victory is oriented toward self. This may seem to be merely splitting hairs over semantics, but there is a subtle, self-centered attitude at the root of many of our difficulties with sin. Until we face this attitude and deal with it, we will not consistently walk in holiness.

This is not to say God doesn't want us to experience victory, but rather to emphasize that victory is a by-product of obedience. As we concentrate on living an obedient, holy life, we will certainly experience the joy of victory over sin.

FAITH OR FLESH?

Our second problem is that we have misunderstood "living by faith" (Galatians 2:20) to mean that no effort at holiness is required on our part. In fact, sometimes we have even suggested that any effort on our part is "of the flesh."

The words of J. C. Ryle, bishop of Liverpool from 1880 to 1900, are instructive to us on this point:

> Is it wise to proclaim in so bald, naked, and unqualified a way as many do, that the holiness of converted people is by faith only, and not at all by personal exertion? Is it according to the proportion of God's Word? I doubt it. That faith in Christ is the root of all holiness…no well-instructed Christian will ever think of denying. But surely the Scriptures teach us that in following holiness the true Christian needs personal exertion and work as well as faith.

We must face the fact that we have a personal responsibility for our walk of holiness. One Sunday our pastor in his sermon said words to this effect: "You can put away that habit that has mastered you if you truly desire to do so." Because he was referring to a particular habit which was no problem to me, I quickly agreed with him in my mind. But then the Holy Spirit said to me, "And you can put away the sinful habits that plague you if you will accept your personal responsibility for them."

Acknowledging that I did have this responsibility turned out to be a milestone for me in my own pursuit of holiness.

THE CREATIVITY OF SIN

Our third problem is that we do not take some sin seriously. We have mentally categorized sin into that which is unacceptable and that which may be tolerated a bit. An incident that occurred illustrates this problem. Our office was using a mobile home as temporary office space, pending the delayed completion of new facilities. Because our property is not zoned for mobile homes, we were required to obtain a variance permit to occupy the trailer. The permit had to be renewed several times. The last permit renewal expired just as the new facilities were completed, but before we had time to move out in an orderly manner. This precipitated a crisis for the department occupying the trailer.

At a meeting where this problem was discussed, the question was asked, "What difference would it make if we didn't move that department for a few days?" Well, what difference would it make? After all, the trailer was tucked in behind some hills where no one would see it. And legally we didn't have to move the trailer, just vacate it. So what difference would it make if we overstayed our permit a few days? Isn't insistence on obeying the letter of the law nitpicking legalism?

But the Scripture says it is "the little foxes that ruin the vineyards" (Song of Songs 2:15, NIV). It is compromise on the little issues that leads to greater downfalls. And who is to say that a little ignoring of civil law is not a serious sin in the sight of God?

WHAT IS THE STANDARD?

In commenting on some of the more minute Old Testament dietary laws God gave to the children of Israel, Andrew Bonar said, "It is not the importance of the thing, but the majesty of the Lawgiver, that is to be the standard of obedience." Some, indeed, might reckon such minute and arbitrary rules as these as trifling. But the principle involved in obedience or disobedience was none other than the same principle which was tried in Eden at the foot of the forbidden tree. It is really this: Is the Lord to be obeyed in all things whatsoever He commands? Is He a holy Lawgiver? Are His creatures bound to give implicit assent to His will?

Are we willing to call sin sin not because it is big or little, but because God's law forbids it? We cannot categorize sin if we are to live a life of holiness. God will not let us get away with that kind of attitude.

STUDY QUESTIONS

1. Take time to settle these issues in your heart right now. Will you begin to look at sin as an offense against a holy God, instead of as only a personal defeat?

2. Will you begin to take personal responsibility for your sin, realizing that as you do, you must depend on the grace of God?

3. Will you decide to obey God in all areas of life, however insignificant the issue may be? List a few areas in which you have not been obedient. How can you take responsibility for these areas?

Chapter 5

The Everyday Business of Holiness

BY CHUCK COLSON

*When godliness is produced in you from the life that is
deep within you—then that godliness is real,
lasting and the genuine essence of the Lord.*

MADAME JEANNE MARIE DE LA MOTHE GUYON

When we think of holiness, great saints of the past
like Francis of Assisi or George Müller spring to
mind—or contemporary giants of the faith like
Mother Teresa. But holiness is not the private preserve of an
elite corps of martyrs, mystics, and Nobel-prize winners.
Holiness is the everyday business of every Christian. It evi-
dences itself in the decisions we make and the things we do,
hour by hour, day by day.

AN EXAMPLE

When she arrives at the prison gate each weekday at noon,
the guards wave her through. Prison officials stop to ask how
her kids are doing or about her work at the office. After all,
Joyce Page is family; she's been spending her lunch hour at

the St. Louis County Correctional Institution just about every weekday since 1979.

Joyce began going to the prison with her supervisor, also a Christian concerned for prisoners. When the supervisor was transferred, Joyce continued by herself, leaving her office alone with a peanut butter sandwich, while other secretaries bustled off in clusters for the cafeteria.

Each day Joyce meets with a different group of inmates, from the men in isolation and maximum security to a small group of women prisoners. "What we do is up to them," she says. "Sometimes we have a worship service, or a time of testimony and singing, or in-depth Bible study and discussion. It depends on their needs."

When she slips back to her desk at one o'clock, one of her coworkers is usually already bemoaning her lunchtime excesses and loudly proclaiming that she really will have the diet plate tomorrow. Joyce laughs to herself. She knows exactly what she'll have for lunch tomorrow—another peanut butter sandwich at the wheel of her car on the way to the prison.

For many, meeting with inmates every day in the middle of a hectic work schedule would be an unthinkable chore. Joyce, in her matter-of-fact way, sees it differently. "For me it's a real answer to prayer," she says. "You see, I don't have time to go *after* work—I have six kids of my own that I'm raising by myself."

Holiness is obeying God—sharing His love, even when it is inconvenient.

HERO VERSUS HOLY

Heroism is an extraordinary feat of the flesh; holiness is an ordinary act of the spirit. One may bring personal glory; the other *always* gives God the glory.

This illustration from Joyce's life can be helpful as a practical example, but the sure standard for holiness is Scripture. There God makes clear what He means by holy living or, as theologians call it, the process of sanctification.

The Ten Commandments, from which all other commandments flow, are the beginning; they apply today as much as they did when God engraved them on tablets of stone for Moses. Next, the life of Jesus provides holiness in the flesh. In His persevering self-denial, His unqualified obedience of the Father's will, and the fullness of the Holy Spirit in His daily life, Jesus remains our example.

The quest for holiness, then, should begin with a search of the Scriptures. We next begin applying what we find, seeking His will for our lives. As the nineteenth-century Scottish theologian John Brown put it: "Holiness does not consist in mystic speculations, enthusiastic fervors, or uncommanded austerities; it consists in thinking as *God* thinks and willing as *God* wills."

That thinking and willing is a process requiring discipline and perseverance and is a joint effort: God's and ours. On the one hand, the Holy Spirit convicts of sin and sanctifies. But that doesn't mean that we can sit back, relax, and leave the driving to God. God expects—demands—that we do our part. As Mother Teresa said, "Our progress in holiness depends on God and ourselves—on God's grace and on our will to be holy."

CLEARING THE WATERS

Understanding this joint responsibility makes clear what is otherwise one of the most troublesome areas for many Christians, found in Paul's letter to the church at Rome, where on one hand he says we are dead to sin and in the next verse exhorts us not to let sin reign in our mortal bodies.

Why should we turn away from sin that is already dead? The answer to this seeming contradiction underscores the joint responsibility for sanctification. We are dead to sin because Christ died to sin for us. He settled the ultimate victory. But as we live day by day, sin still remains a constant reality. Though God gives us the will to be holy, the daily fight requires continuing effort on our part.

Holy living demands constant examination of our actions and motives. But in doing so, we must guard against the tendency to focus totally on self, which is easy to do—especially as the culture's egocentric values invade the church. In fact, this self-indulgent character of our times is a major reason the topic of true holiness is so neglected today by Christian teachers, leaders, writers, and speakers. We have, perhaps unconsciously, substituted a secularized, self-centered message in its place. For when we speak of "victory" in the Christian life, we all too often mean personal victory—how God will conquer sin for us (at least those sins we would like to be rid of, such as those extra ten pounds, that annoying habit, maybe a quick temper). This reflects not only egocentricity, but an incorrect view of sin.

COSMIC TREASON

Sin is not simply the wrong we do our neighbor when we cheat him, or the wrong we do ourselves when we abuse our bodies. Sin—all sin—is a root rebellion and offense against God, what R. C. Sproul calls "cosmic treason."

We must understand that our goal as believers is to seek what we can do to please God, not what He can do for us. Personal victories may come, but they are a result, not the object. True Christian maturity—holiness, sanctification—is God-centered. So-called "victorious Christian living" is self-centered. Jerry Bridges puts it well:

> It is time for us Christians to face up to our responsibility for holiness. Too often we say we are "defeated" by this or that sin. No, we are not defeated; we are simply disobedient. It might be well if we stopped using the terms "victory" and "defeat" to describe our progress in holiness. Rather we should use the terms "obedience" and "disobedience."

So we have come full circle—back to where we started. The Christian life begins with obedience, depends on obedience, and results in obedience. We can't escape it.

IT'S ALL ABOUT OBEDIENCE

A young woman in a suburban Washington church recently demonstrated this truth.

No one was surprised when Patti Awan stood during the informal praise time at the Sunday-evening service. A young Sunday-school teacher with an air of quiet maturity, she had given birth to a healthy son a few months earlier, a first child for her and her husband, Javy. The congregation settled back for a report of the baby's progress and his parents' thanksgiving. They were totally unprepared for what followed.

Hanging on to the podium before her, Patti began. "Four years ago this week, a young girl sat crying on the floor of a New Jersey apartment, devastated by the news of a lab report. Unmarried and alone, she had just learned she was pregnant."

The congregation grew completely quiet; Patti's tear-choked voice indicated just who that young woman was.

"I considered myself a Christian at the time," she continued. "But I had found out about Christ while in the drug scene. After I learned about Him, I knew I wanted to commit myself to Him, but I couldn't give up my old friends or my old habits. So I was drifting between two worlds—in one, still smoking dope every day and sleeping with the man who lived in the apartment below mine; in the other, going to church, witnessing to others, and working with the church youth group.

"But being pregnant ripped through the hypocrisy of my double life. I had been meaning to 'get right with God,' but I kept slipping back. Now I couldn't live a nice, clean Christian life like all those church people.

"I felt the only answer was to wipe the slate clean. I would get an abortion; no one in the church would ever know.

"The clinic scheduled an abortion date. I was terrified, but my boyfriend was adamant. My sister was furious with me for being so stupid as to get pregnant. Finally, in desperation I wrote my parents. They were staunch Catholics, and I knew they would support me if I decided to have the baby. My mother called me: 'If you don't get an abortion, I don't want to see you while you're pregnant. Your life will be ruined, and you'll deserve it.'

"I had always been desperately dependent on other people. But I knew this was one decision I had to make alone. I was looking out my bedroom window one night when I thought clearly for the first time in weeks. I realized I either believed this Christianity or I didn't believe it. And if I believed in Christ, then I couldn't do this. *God is real*, I thought, *even if I've never lived like He is.*

"That decision was a point of no return. I put my faith in the God of the Bible, not the God I had made up in my head.

I was still everything I never wanted to be: pregnant, alone, deserted by family, and rejected by the one I had loved. Yet for the first time in my life I was really peaceful, because I knew for the first time I was being obedient.

"When I went to an obstetrician and told him of my decision to have the baby and why I had made that choice, he refused to charge me for the prenatal care and delivery. I confessed my double life to the church, and through the support of Christians was able to move away from my old friends to an apartment of my own. I began going to a Christian counseling agency and felt God leading me to give the baby up for adoption.

"I had a beautiful baby girl and named her Sarah. She was placed with a childless Christian couple, and we all felt God's hand in the decision.

"And so that's why I praise God this evening. I thought in the depths of my despair that my life was ruined, but I knew I had to at least be obedient in taking responsibility for my sin. But today, because of that very despair and obedience, I have what I never thought I could: a godly husband and now a baby of our own. But what matters more than anything is that I have what I was searching for so desperately before: peace with God."

Holiness is obeying God.

Study Questions

1. In what areas of your life are you demonstrating holiness on a daily basis?

2. In what areas of your life are you demonstrating a more self-centered attitude?

3. In Hebrews 5, the writer exhorts his readers to move past an immature spiritual diet of milk and move on to a spiritual diet of meat so that they might be teachers of the Word. What do you need to change about your spiritual diet that would help you reach this spiritual maturity?

Taken from *Loving God*, by Charles Colson. Copyright © 1983, 1987, 1996 by Charles W. Colson. Used by permission of Zondervan.

Chapter 6

Absolute Surrender

By Andrew Murray

And Ben-hadad the king of Syria gathered all his host together: and there
were thirty and two kings with him, and horses, and chariots:
and he went up and besieged Samaria, and warred against it.
And he sent messengers to Ahab king of Israel into the city, and said
unto him, Thus saith Ben-hadad, Thy silver and thy gold is mine; thy
wives also and thy children, even the goodliest, are mine. And the king of
Israel answered and said, My lord, O king, according to thy saying,
I am thine, and all that I have.

1 KINGS 20:1–4, KJV

What Ben-hadad asked was absolute surrender, and
Ahab gave what was asked of him—*absolute sur-*
render. I want to use these words, "My lord, O
king, according to thy saying, I am thine, and all that I have,"
as the words of absolute surrender with which every child of
God ought to yield himself to his Father. If our hearts are willing for that, there is no end to what God will do for us, and
to the blessing God will bestow.

Absolute surrender. Let me tell you where I got that term.
In Scotland, I was in a company where we were talking about
the condition of Christ's church, and what the great need of

the church and of believers is. There was in our company one who has much to do in training Christian workers, and I asked him what he would say was the great need of the church. He answered simply and determinedly: "Absolute surrender to God is the one thing."

The words struck me as never before. And that man began to tell how, in the workers with whom he had to deal, he finds that if they are sound on that point, even though they be backward, they are willing to be taught and helped, and they always improve; whereas, others who are not sound there very often go back and leave the work. The condition for obtaining God's full blessing is *absolute surrender* to Him.

ARE YOU WILLING?

Now, God in heaven answers the prayers which you have offered for blessing on yourselves and for blessing around you by this one demand: Are you willing to surrender yourself absolutely into His hands? What is our answer to be?

Let me say, first of all, *God claims it from us*. Yes, it has its foundation in the very nature of God. God cannot do otherwise.

Who is God? He is the Fountain of life, the only Source of existence and power and goodness, and throughout the universe there is nothing good but what God works. God has created the sun, and the moon, and the stars, and the flowers, and the trees, and the grass; and are they not all absolutely surrendered to God? Do they not allow God to work in them just what He pleases? When God clothes the lily with its beauty, is it not yielded up, surrendered, given over to God as He works in it its beauty?

And God's redeemed children, oh, can you think that God can work His work if there is only half or a part of them surrendered? God is life, and love, and blessing, and power, and infinite beauty, and God delights to communicate Himself to every child who is prepared to receive Him. But this one lack of absolute surrender is just the thing that hinders God. And now He comes and as God He claims it.

GOD'S AT THE HELM

But, secondly, God not only claims it, but *God will work it Himself*. I am sure there is many a heart that says, "Ah, but that absolute surrender implies so much!" A little while ago I had an appealing little note in which the writer said, "I have passed through so much trial and suffering, and there is so much of the self-life still remaining and I dare not face the entire giving of it up, because I know it will cause so much trouble and agony." Alas! Alas that God's children have such thoughts of Him, such cruel thoughts!

God does not ask you to give the perfect surrender in your strength, or by the power of your will: God is willing to work it in you. Do we not read, "It is God that worketh in us, both to will and to do of His good pleasure"? Believe that the everlasting God Himself will come into your heart, to turn out what is wrong, to conquer what is evil, and to work what is well-pleasing in His blessed sight. God Himself will work it in you.

Look at the men in the Old Testament, like Abraham. Do you think it was by accident that God found that man, the father of the faithful and the friend of God, and that it was Abraham himself, apart from God, who had such faith and such obedience and devotion?

You know it is not so. God raised him up, and prepared him as an instrument for His glory. Did not God say to Pharaoh, "For this cause have I raised thee up, for to show in thee My power"? And if God said that of him, will not God say it far more of every child of His?

HIS WONDERFUL MERCY

The third thought. God not only claims it and works it, but *God accepts it when we bring it to Him.* God works it in the secret of our heart. God urges us by the hidden power of His Holy Spirit to come and speak it out, and we have to bring and to yield to Him that absolute surrender.

And if you say, "Lord, I yield myself in absolute surrender," even though it be with a trembling heart and with the consciousness, "I do not feel the power, I do not feel the determination, I do not feel the assurance," it will succeed. Even in the midst of your trembling, the power of the Holy Ghost will work.

Have you never yet learned the lesson that the Holy Ghost works with mighty power, while on the human side everything appears feeble? Look at the Lord Jesus Christ in Gethsemane. We read that He "through the eternal Spirit" offered Himself a sacrifice unto God. The almighty Spirit of God was enabling Him to do it. Yet what agony and fear and exceeding sorrow came over Him, and how He prayed! Externally you can see no sign of the mighty power of the Spirit, but the Spirit of God was there. And even so, while you are feeble and fighting and trembling, in faith in the hidden work of God's Spirit, do not fear, but yield yourself.

NOT MY STRENGTH

A fourth thought. God not only claims it, and works it, and accepts it when I bring it, but *God maintains it.* That is the great difficulty with many. You may say, "I have often been stirred at a meeting, or at a convention and I have consecrated myself to God, but it has passed away. I know it may last for a week or for a month, but away it fades, and after a time it is all gone."

It is because you do not believe that when God has begun the work of absolute surrender in you, and when God has accepted your surrender, then God holds Himself bound to care for it and to keep it.

In this matter of surrender there are two, *God and I*—I a worm, God the everlasting and omnipotent Jehovah. Worm, will you be afraid to trust yourself to this mighty God? God is willing.

If God allows the sun to shine upon you moment by moment, without intermission, will not God let His life shine upon you every moment? And why have you not experienced it? Because you have not trusted God for it, and you do not surrender yourself absolutely to God in that trust.

A life of absolute surrender has its difficulties. I do not deny that. Yea, it has something far more than difficulties. It is a life that with men is absolutely impossible. But by the grace of God, by the power of God, by the power of the Holy Spirit dwelling in us, it is a life to which we are destined, and a life that is possible for us. Let us believe that God will maintain it.

On his ninetieth birthday, George Müller was asked the secret of his happiness, and of all the blessing with which God had visited him. He said he believed there were two reasons. The one was that he had been enabled by grace to maintain a good conscience before God day by day; the other was that he was a lover of God's Word. A good conscience in unfeigned obedience to God day by day; and fellowship with God every day in His Word, and prayer—that is a life of absolute surrender.

Reaping the Rewards

The last thought. This absolute surrender to God *will wonderfully bless us.* What Ahab said to his enemy, King Ben-hadad— "My lord, O king, according to thy word I am thine, and all that I have"—shall we not say to our God and loving Father? If we do say it, God's blessing will come upon us. God wants you to be separate from the world; you are called to come out from the world that hates God. Come out for God and say, "Lord, anything for Thee." If you say that with prayer, and speak that into God's ear, He will accept it, and He will teach you what it means.

I repeat, God will bless you. You have been praying for blessing. But do remember, there must be absolute surrender. At every tea table you see it. Why is tea poured into that cup? Because it is empty, and given up for the tea. But put ink, or vinegar, or wine into it, and will they pour the tea into the vessel? And can God fill you, can God bless you, if you are not absolutely surrendered to Him? He cannot. Believe that God has wonderful blessings for you, if you will but say, be it with a trembling will, yet with a believing heart, "O God, I accept Thy demands, I am Thine, and all that I have. Absolute surrender is what my soul yields Thee, by divine grace."

You may not have such strong and clear feelings of deliverance as you would desire to have; but humble yourselves in His sight, and acknowledge that you have grieved the Holy Spirit by your self-will, self-confidence, and self-effort. Bow humbly before Him in the confession of that, and ask Him to break the heart and to bring you into the dust before Him. Then, as you bow before Him, just accept God's teaching that in your flesh "there dwelleth no good thing," and that nothing will help you except another life which must come in. You must deny self once for all. Denying self must every moment be the power of your life, and then Christ will come in and take possession of you.

STUDY QUESTIONS

1. In God's eyes, halfhearted devotion is an oxymoron. Even Jesus said it is better to be cold or hot than lukewarm. So where does that leave you? Are you wholly devoted to God?

2. Are you willing to pray to God the words of Ahab: "My Lord, O King, according to Thy saying, I am Thine, and all that I have"?

3. Take a moment to reflect on the consequences of absolute surrender to God. Before you pray the words of Ahab, count the cost. Then pray as God leads.

Taken from *Absolute Surrender,* by Andrew Murray. Copyright © by Christian Literature Crusade. Used by permission.

Chapter 7

Feeding on the Word of God

BY JACK HAYFORD

I study my Bible as I gather apples. First, I shake the whole tree that the ripest might fall. Then I shake each limb, and when I have shaken each limb, I shake each branch and every twig. Then I look under every leaf.

MARTIN LUTHER

To begin, we all know and agree: The Word of God is absolutely essential to our personal lives, and it will only find its place there on the basis of our making a choice to read it daily and exercising that duty.

No argument. As we look into the place of the Word in our private devotional life, may I share with you a simple, personal guideline that I have found? It's worked for decades in my Christian walk, and I've recommended it to thousands. How I keep from failing to read God's Word every day: I simply don't turn out the light. That's right. I've connected that last action of the day to becoming "impossible" without reading the Word. It's as though I'm saying, "This light doesn't go out until this Light goes in!"

Of course, you may employ other means, patterns, reminders, and times. Many read the Word first thing in the morning, and I'm often there with them, too. But at a personal dimension, I found that in the morning I often was too tempted to substitute devotional reading of the Word for devotional time in prayer with the Lord. So I usually read the Bible in the evening.

Nonetheless, the issue is that we establish the habit. The time and the coverage is yours to establish. And whatever difficulty you may have in becoming a faithful Bible reader, press forward. It's a most essential discipline to master, and we need to establish at least the habit of reading chapters (plural) almost every day.

VALUES IN BIBLE READING HABIT

Look very seriously with me, will you, at why we need the Word of God in our lives. You may want to jot down these key principles on the blank front or back page of your Bible, as a reference point and reminder that God's Word is essential to everything in our lives—every issue of life is covered by truth and wisdom contained in this precious book.

1. God's Word ensures certainty about your path.

> Then I would not be ashamed, when I look into all
> Your commandments. (Psalm 119:6)

The word *ashamed*, as used here, literally means "I won't be embarrassed." In short, I'm not going to come up short when "I have respect unto all Your Word, Lord." His Word will help me avoid confusion and embarrassing stumbling around with my life.

2. *God's Word gives direction about your path.*

Your word is a lamp to my feet and a light to my path.
(Psalm 119:105)

Of course, simply giving place to the Word of God every day is taking an oath of allegiance: "Lord, Your Word is foundational and prior in all matters of my life." This acknowledgment brings certain direction.

In all your ways acknowledge Him, and He shall direct your paths. (Proverbs 3:6)

Notice too that the direction which comes from God's Word is both immediately at hand, as well as revealing that which is distant. When the Bible says, "Your Word is a lamp and a light," the Hebrew words are the equivalent in today's technology to saying, "You'll have a flashlight in one hand and a giant spotlight in the other." Both aspects of my pathway come into view: details for today and discernment for tomorrow.

3. *God's Word gives wisdom about your path.*

The law of the LORD is perfect, converting the soul;
the testimony of the LORD is sure, making wise the simple. (Psalm 19:7)

The word *simple* makes an honest reference to an "inexperienced" person, and is not a condescending slur, as though the person were being stupid or ignorant. Just as the Bible points the way to wisdom both for today's immediate situation and for the long-range path we're to pursue, here the Word is promised as a resource to assure wisdom for things we face in which we have no experience. This doesn't mean that every question we face finds an immediate answer. It means as I feed on the Word daily, the wisdom I need for living my life will distill in my soul. Let me elaborate.

I've learned that regular reading seldom gives me a "shot" of perceived wisdom each day. But I've found, nonetheless, that the Holy Spirit has a way of causing me to receive wisdom as a deposit; not so much in phrases or words, but in the elements of wisdom, the nutrients of God's truth, flowing into my spirit. Then, when I need it, though I may not remember chapters and verses, the strength and wisdom needed will be available by reason of the spiritual resources inside—that which has accumulated through faithfulness to this spiritual habit.

Sometime back, a friend of my mother's said to her, "Dolores, I feel so stupid when I study the Word of God. I just don't seem to remember anything at all."

Quite wisely, my mother said, "Lou, do you remember what you ate for breakfast on Tuesday, three weeks ago?"

She looked at her rather stunned and replied, "Well, no, I don't."

Mama explained, "It still supported and nourished you, didn't it?"

Get the point? Just keep reading the Bible. You may not remember everything, but the Word is flowing into your spirit, and as it does, it's giving abiding strength to sustain you. Simply obey—and read.

Jesus said, "Man shall not live by bread alone, but by every word that proceeds from the mouth of God" (Matthew 4:4). There is your daily bread! We can expect strength today, not only because of today's reading, but there's also a component of strength by reason of what we "ate" Tuesday, three weeks ago, when we fed on the Word of God!

4. *God's Word ensures our victory in our pathway.*

This Book of the Law shall not depart from your mouth, but you shall meditate in it day and night, that you may observe to do according to all that is written in it. For then you will make your way prosperous, and then you will have good success. (Joshua 1:8)

Praise the Lord! Listen, there's something about giving place to the Word of God that ensures not only today's nourishment but also our success!

Joshua had just taken over the leadership reins of responsibility from Moses, following the latter's death. Can you imagine the impossible challenge this was from Joshua's viewpoint? But God gave Joshua the promise of His presence and His purpose, linking them to His precepts.

The promise of success, through God's promised presence and unfolding purpose being realized in our life, is offered today on the same terms as to Joshua. Keep the Word in your mind, in your heart, and on your lips! The Word works—richly and mightily:

Let the word of Christ dwell in you richly in all wisdom.... According to His working which works in me mightily. (Colossians 3:16; 1:29)

So the word of the Lord grew mightily and prevailed. (Acts 19:20)

5. *God's Word keeps us pure in our path.*

How can a young man cleanse his way? By taking heed according to Your word. (Psalm 119:9)

Your word I have hidden in my heart, that I might not sin against You. (Psalm 119:11)

Another value of reading the Bible is the power of the Word to keep us pure. It's not just a spotlight which shines outward and gives direction; it's a searchlight which shines inward—prompting, correcting, adjusting, and instructing me. Jesus prayed, "[Father,] sanctify them by Your truth. Your word is truth" (John 17:17). He also declared, "And you shall know the truth, and the truth shall make you free" (John 8:32). God's Word not only purifies from sin, it is a preventative against sin!

In every instance when Jesus faced temptation in the wilderness, as Satan came not only to taunt but to destroy Him, Jesus responded to each thrust of the adversary's lies with a counterthrust of the sword of the Spirit: the truth of the Word of God.

D. L. Moody said of God's Word, "This Book will keep you from sin, or sin will keep you from this Book." So today we have the Bible not only as a "Resource Book" to give certainty, direction, wisdom, and victory, but we have it as a "Resistance Book" for keeping us pure.

6. God's Word keeps us alert to the times.

And everyone who has this hope in Him purifies himself, just as He is pure. (1 John 3:3)

The Scriptures sometimes glare with flashing warning signs showing the nature of our times, and signaling us to stay readied for Jesus Christ's return. With our eyes on the Lord—"loving His appearing"—the Word is key to keeping us sensitive, keeping us from falling asleep as the darkening hour and spirit of our age could lull us into carnal sleepiness or sensual indulgence. The Word will keep us walking a pure path and maintaining an alert stance, strong and ready to do battle in the name of the Lord.

The promise of Jesus' soon return is real! And steadfast, daily, heartwarming, self-examining, faith-building, soul-purifying reading is a key to "keeping ready."

7. God's Word is our shield of faith.

> So then faith comes by hearing, and hearing by the word of God. (Romans 10:17)

Our faith is our fundamental means to resist the devil—the shield we use to withstand him. Faith defends against attack as an implement which is forged and fashioned in one way: by our "hearing" the Word of God.

But remember, fellow-learner, "hearing" is not a passive sit-in-church-once-weekly-and-you're-done proposition. Rather, to "hear" the Word is 1) to feed on it as a steadfast practice, and 2) to heed it as a sensitive "hearer." The starting place for life-growing faith is in the heeding to reading—obeying His leading unto feeding as one of Jesus' sheep. That's what will bring fullness of faith and build us as victors, from a sheep to a soldier!

Feed and heed! That's our call to this "Resource above all resources," the Standard by which everything is gauged, the Foundational Footing for everywhere you may walk in life—the living, eternal, holy Word of God.

Live *in* it.
Live *by* it.
Live *through* it.
Daily.

STUDY QUESTIONS

1. How does the Word of God give you "wisdom about your path"?

2. How does the reading of God's Word help you overcome temptation?

3. Do you have a time set aside to read the Bible? If not, do so now and make a commitment to not "turn out the light" (or move on to your next thing) until you've read at least one chapter. Once it's a habit, try to work up to several chapters a day.

Taken from *Living the Spirit Formed Life,* by Jack Hayford. Copyright © 2001. Gospel Light/Regal Books, Ventura, CA 93003. Used by permission.

Chapter 8

Train Yourself to Be Godly

BY JERRY BRIDGES

*Have nothing to do with godless myths and old wives' tales;
rather, train yourself to be godly.*

1 TIMOTHY 4:7, NIV

The apostle Paul did not take for granted the godliness of his spiritual son Timothy. Though Timothy had been his companion and colaborer for a number of years, Paul still felt it necessary to write to him, "Train yourself to be godly." And if Timothy needed this encouragement, then surely we also need it today.

In urging Timothy to train himself in godliness, Paul borrowed a term from the realm of athletics. The verb which is variously translated in different versions of the Bible as *exercise, discipline,* or *train* originally referred to the training of young athletes for participation in the competitive games of the day. Then it took on a more general meaning of training or discipline of either the body or the mind in a particular skill.

PRINCIPLES FOR TRAINING

There are several principles in Paul's exhortation to Timothy to train himself to be godly that are applicable to us today. The first is *personal responsibility*. Paul said, "Train yourself." Timothy was personally responsible for his progress in godliness. He was not to trust the Lord for that progress and then relax, though he certainly understood that any progress he made was only through divine enablement. He would have understood that he was to work out this particular aspect of his salvation in confidence that God was at work in him. But he would see Paul's message that he must work at this matter of godliness; he must *pursue* it.

We Christians may be very disciplined and industrious in our business, our studies, our home, or even our ministry, but we tend to be lazy when it comes to exercise in our own spiritual lives. We would much rather pray, "Lord, make me godly," and expect Him to "pour" some godliness into our souls in some mysterious way. God does, in fact, work in a mysterious way to make us godly, but He does not do this apart from the fulfillment of our own personal responsibility. We are to train ourselves to be godly.

The second principle in Paul's exhortation is that *the object of this training was growth in Timothy's personal spiritual life*. Elsewhere Paul encourages Timothy to progress in his ministry, but the objective here is Timothy's own devotion to God and the conduct arising from that devotion. Even though he was an experienced, well-qualified Christian minister, Timothy still needed to grow in the essential areas of godliness: the fear of God, the comprehension of the love of God, and the desire for the presence and fellowship of God.

I have been in a full-time Christian ministry for well over twenty-five years and have served both overseas and in the

United States. During this time, I have met many talented and capable Christians, but I think I have met fewer godly Christians. The emphasis of our age is on serving God, accomplishing things for God. Enoch was a preacher of righteousness in a day of gross ungodliness, but God saw fit that the brief account of his life emphasized that he walked with God. What are we training ourselves for? Are we training ourselves only in Christian activity, as good as that may be, or are we training ourselves first of all in godliness?

The third principle in Paul's words of exhortation to Timothy is the importance of *minimum characteristics necessary for training.* Many of us have watched various Olympic competitions on television, and as the commentators have given us the backgrounds of the various athletes, we become aware of certain irreducible minimums in the training of all Olympic competitors. It is very likely that Paul had these minimum characteristics in mind as he compared physical training with training in godliness.

THE COST OF COMMITMENT

The first of these irreducible minimums is *commitment.* No one makes it to the level of Olympic, or even national, competition without a commitment to pay the price of rigorous daily training. And similarly, no one ever becomes godly without a commitment to pay the price of the daily spiritual training which God has designed for our growth in godliness.

The concept of commitment occurs repeatedly throughout the Bible. It is found in David's cry to God: "Earnestly I seek you" (Psalm 63:1, NIV). It is found in God's promise to the captives in Babylon: "You will seek me and find me when you seek me with all your heart" (Jeremiah 29:13, NIV). It occurs in Paul's pressing on to take hold of that for which

Christ Jesus took hold of him (Philippians 3:12). It lies behind such exhortations as, "Make every effort...to be holy" (Hebrews 12:14, NIV) and, "Make every effort to add to your faith...godliness" (2 Peter 1:5, 7, NIV). None of this seeking, pressing on, or making every effort will occur without commitment on our part.

There is a price to godliness, and godliness is never on sale. It never comes cheaply or easily. The verb *train,* which Paul deliberately chose, implies persevering, painstaking, diligent effort. He was well aware of the total commitment those young athletes made to win a crown that would not last. And as he thought of the crown that would last—the godliness that has value for all things, both in the present life and the life to come—he urged Timothy, and he urges us today, to make the kind of commitment necessary to train ourselves to be godly.

LEARNING FROM A SKILLED TEACHER

The second irreducible minimum in training is a *competent teacher or coach.* No athlete, regardless of how much natural ability he has, can make it to the Olympics without a skillful coach who holds him to the highest standard of excellence and sees and corrects every minor fault. In the same way, we cannot train ourselves to be godly without the teaching and training ministry of the Holy Spirit. He holds us to the highest standard of spiritual excellence as He teaches, rebukes, corrects, and trains us. But He teaches and trains us through His Word. Therefore, we must consistently expose ourselves to the teaching of the Word of God if we are to grow in godliness.

In Titus 1:1 (NIV), Paul refers to "the knowledge of the truth that leads to godliness." We cannot grow in godliness without the knowledge of this truth. This truth is to be found only in the Bible, but it is not just academic knowledge of Bible facts. It is spiritual knowledge taught by the Holy Spirit as He applies the truth of God to our hearts.

There is a type of religious knowledge that is actually detrimental to training in godliness. It is the knowledge that puffs up with spiritual pride. The Corinthian Christians had this kind of knowledge. They knew that an idol was nothing and that eating food sacrificed to an idol was a matter of spiritual indifference. But they did not know about their responsibility to love their weaker brother. Only the Holy Spirit imparts that type of knowledge—the type that leads to godliness.

It is possible to be very orthodox in one's doctrine and very upright in one's behavior and still not be godly. Many people are orthodox and upright, but they are not devoted to God; they are devoted to their orthodoxy and their standards of moral conduct.

Only the Holy Spirit can pry us loose from such positions of false confidence, so we must sincerely look to Him for His training ministry as we seek to grow in godliness. We must spend much time in exposure to His Word, since it is His means of teaching us. But this exposure must be accompanied by a sense of deep humility regarding our ability to learn spiritual truth, and a sense of utter dependence upon His ministry in our hearts.

PRACTICE AND MORE PRACTICE

The third irreducible minimum in the training process is *practice*. It is practice that puts feet to the commitment and applies the teaching of the coach. It is practice, where the skill is developed, that makes the athlete competitive in his sport.

And it is the practice of godliness that enables us to become godly Christians. There is no shortcut to Olympic-level skill; there is no shortcut to godliness. It is the day-in and day-out faithfulness to the means which God has appointed and which the Holy Spirit uses that will enable us to grow in godliness. We must *practice* godliness, just as the athlete practices his particular sport.

We must practice the fear of God, for example, if we are to grow in that aspect of godly devotion. If we agree that the essential elements of the fear of God are correct concepts of His character, a pervasive sense of His presence, and a constant awareness of our responsibility to Him, then we must work at filling our minds with the biblical expressions of these truths and applying them in our lives until we are transformed into God-fearing people.

If we become convinced that humility is a trait of godly character, then we will frequently meditate upon such Scripture passages as Isaiah 57:15 and 66:1–2, where God Himself extols humility. We will pray over them, asking the Holy Spirit to apply them in our lives to make us truly humble. This is the practice of godliness. It is not some ethereal exercise. It is practical, down-to-earth, and even a bit grubby at times, as the Holy Spirit works on us. But it is always rewarding as we see the Spirit transforming us more and more into godly people.

THE NATURE OF TRAINING

Paul said, "Train yourself to be godly." You and I are responsible to train ourselves. We are dependent upon God for His divine enablement, but we are responsible; we are not passive in this process. Our objective in this process is godliness— not proficiency in ministry, but God-centered devotion and

Godlike character. We do want to develop proficiency in ministry, but for training in godliness we want to focus on our relationship with God.

Training in godliness requires commitment, the teaching ministry of the Holy Spirit through His Word, and practice on our part. Are we prepared to accept our responsibility and make that commitment? As we ponder that question, let us remember, "Godliness has value for all things, holding promise for both the present life and the life to come," and "Godliness with contentment is great gain" (1 Timothy 4:8; 6:6, NIV).

STUDY QUESTIONS

1. What are the three principles Paul uses to exhort Timothy to godliness?

2. Of the three "irreducible minimums" Paul cites, which one is most evident in your life? Least evident?

3. What is your answer to this question: "Are you prepared to accept your responsibility and make the commitment to train for godliness?"

Reprinted from *The Practice of Godliness,* by Jerry Bridges. Copyright © 1983, 1996 by Jerry Bridges. Used by permission of NavPress, Colorado Springs, CO. All rights reserved.

Chapter 9

We Grow Through Exercise

BY WARREN WIERSBE

God wants worshipers before workers;
indeed the only acceptable workers are those who
have learned the lost art of worship.

A. W. TOZER

*N*ourishment without exercise will make a person overweight, sluggish, and fair game for a variety of physical problems. What's true of the body is also true of the inner person: Unless we devote ourselves to spiritual exercise, the nourishment we take will probably do us more harm than good. Too many saints are overfed and underexercised, and that's why Paul tied food and exercise together when he wrote these words to Timothy:

> If you instruct the brethren in these things, you will
> be a good minister of Jesus Christ, nourished in the
> words of faith and of the good doctrine which you
> have carefully followed. But reject profane and old
> wives' fables, and exercise yourself toward godliness.

For bodily exercise profits a little, but godliness is profitable for all things, having promise of the life that now is and of that which is to come. (1 Timothy 4:6–8)

EXERCISING SELF-CONTROL

The word *exercise,* like the word *discipline,* irritates some people, particularly those who prefer to saunter their way through life indulging in pleasure rather than investing in character. "Whenever I think about exercising," said a contemporary wit, "I just sit down and rest until the feeling goes away." The fact that one day he may sit down and never stand up again probably never enters his mind.

Whether it's playing a musical instrument, mastering a computer program, or learning a foreign language, any worthwhile endeavor demands discipline and exercise. Aristotle called self-control "the hardest victory," and he was probably right. Until we learn how to exercise self-control, we aren't likely to learn anything else that's important to a successful life. We must exercise discipline even to sit still and read a book or listen to somebody teach.

There was a time in church history when believers delighted to discuss the spiritual disciplines of the Christian life, but today anything that smacks of discipline is branded as "legalistic" and alien to the New Testament emphasis on grace. Contemporary Christians don't have time for spiritual disciplines such as worship, fasting, prayer, meditation, self-examination, and confession. We're too busy running to meetings and looking for guaranteed shortcuts to maturity.

Some of today's Christians remind me of the millions of fans who crowd the sports arenas and stadiums week after week, cheering their favorite teams to victory. After each game, these fans shout, "We won! We won!" when in reality the athletes did both the playing and the winning. All the fans did was pay for a ticket, fill a seat, and make a lot of noise. The spectators, not the players, are the ones who really need the exercise; but they settle for shouting, "We won!" and claiming the credit that belongs only to the disciplined athletes.

It doesn't take much effort to be a successful spectator, but we must remember that spectators don't experience the joy that comes with being disciplined, working with teammates, and giving their best; nor do spectators win any awards. Too many evangelical church services are attended by enthusiastic people who buy their tickets (the offering), watch the game (the service), and cheer when there is victory (people responding). They know little or nothing about exercising the disciplines that transform spectators into winning athletes who glorify God.

If you want to be a child of God who does more than watch and cheer, you'll have to learn the disciplines of the Christian life. You'll have to become a disciple. Disciples are believers who practice discipline. They understand spiritual exercise.

DEDICATING OURSELVES

Our most important spiritual exercise, and perhaps the most difficult to learn, is worship. Everything we are and everything we do in the Christian life flows out of worship. Jesus said, "Without Me you can do nothing" (John 15:5).

What is worship? To someone brought up in the Quaker tradition, worship might mean waiting quietly before the Lord and listening for His word in the silence; to a charismatic believer, worship might imply a more enthusiastic expression of praise and adoration. I think that the definition of worship by William Temple covers the essential elements involved in personal and corporate worship:

> For worship is the submission of all our nature to God. It is the quickening of conscience by His holiness; the nourishment of mind with His truth; the purifying of imagination by His beauty; the opening of the heart to His love; the surrender of will to His purpose—and all of this gathered up in adoration, the most selfless emotion of which our nature is capable and therefore the chief remedy for that self-centeredness which is our original sin and the source of all actual sin.

Paul wrote, "I beseech you therefore, brethren, by the mercies of God, that you present your bodies a living sacrifice, holy, acceptable to God, which is your reasonable service [spiritual act of worship (NIV)]" (Romans 12:1).

When you give your body to the Lord, you give Him all the elements mentioned in Temple's definition of worship because the word *body* includes the whole person—the conscience, mind, imagination, heart, will, and all the faculties, talents, and gifts inhabiting that holy temple.

The tense of the verb *present* indicates a once-and-for-all step of faith, as we present ourselves to the Lord in a solemn act of dedication. But I like to renew that dedication at the beginning of each day. It's like the bride and groom at the marriage altar: They give themselves to each other once and for all, but they belong to each other for the rest of their lives. The wedding dedication only introduces them to the marriage devotion, which should get richer as the years pass. Any married couple that tries to live on the memories of a beautiful wedding, without cultivating a deepening relationship of love, doesn't understand what marriage is all about.

PRAISING AND MEDITATING

Worship involves not only *presentation* but also *adoration* as we offer our spiritual sacrifices of praise and thanksgiving to God: "Therefore by Him let us continually offer the sacrifice of praise to God, that is, the fruit of our lips, giving thanks to His name" (Hebrews 13:15). Whether we praise Him by using one of the Psalms, a text from the hymnal, something spontaneous from the heart, or perhaps all three, we ought to focus our full attention on Him and Him alone. David expressed his praise this way: "Bless the LORD, O my soul; and all that is within me, bless His holy name!" (Psalm 103:1).

Worship also includes *meditation,* reading the Word of God, thinking about it, praying over it, asking the Spirit to show us Christ and teach us the truth and then help us apply the truth to our own lives. This is what William Temple calls "the nourishment of mind with His truth." All that we need to know about God will be given to us in the Scriptures; and the better we know Him, the more we will love Him.

PRAYER

Worship must include *prayer.*

Jesus didn't give His followers a philosophy of prayer or even a theology of prayer. Instead, He gave them an example of prayer as they watched His own prayer life; He told them encouraging parables about prayer; and He taught them a model prayer to guide them in their praying. What we call the Lord's Prayer is the inspired pattern for us to follow as we pray:

Our Father in heaven, hallowed be Your name. Your kingdom come. Your will be done on earth as it is in heaven. Give us this day our daily bread. And forgive us our debts, as we forgive our debtors. And do not lead us into temptation, but deliver us from the evil one. (Matthew 6:9–13)

The first thing that strikes you about this prayer is that it uses *only plural pronouns* when referring to God's people. It's not "My Father" but "Our Father"; it's not "Give me" but "Give us." This prayer is a family prayer that involves all the people of God. In fact, a dual relationship is expressed with "Our Father": a relationship with other believers ("Our"), and a relationship with God ("Father").

As a child of God, I can pray in solitude, but I can never pray alone. I must consider other believers as well. I must keep before me all the family of God and not pray for anything for myself that would in any way harm one of God's children. The blessings that come to me in answer to prayer must also bring blessing to the rest of God's family. James said that one reason God's children were at war with each other was because their praying was selfish (James 4:1–3). They were praying "My Father" instead of "Our Father."

Prayer involves relationships, and it also involves *responsibilities:* the glory of God's name ("Hallowed be Your name"), the success of God's kingdom ("Your kingdom come"), and the fulfilling of God's will ("Your will be done"). Before we even pray about our own concerns, we must focus on the concerns of God. I dare not ask anything of the Father that would dishonor His name, hinder the coming of His kingdom, or obstruct the fulfilling of His will on earth.

Why are God's concerns put ahead of my personal needs

and requests? First of all, because they're far more important than any needs I may have. Second, they are put first so that I can evaluate my prayers and see if they are truly a part of what God is doing in this world. As Robert Law said, "The purpose of prayer is not to get man's will done in heaven, but to get God's will done on earth."

If my relationships are right with God and God's family, and if I sincerely accept the responsibilities that go along with being a praying Christian, then I'm ready to come to the Father with my *requests*. These include daily bread, forgiveness, and protection from the evil one.

Daily bread includes every need I have in *the present* ("this day"), whether it's food to eat, clothes to wear, money to pay my bills, or the strength to get through a difficult day. Forgiveness looks to *the past* and deals with whatever God has on my record that needs to be wiped clean (1 John 1:9). Deliverance relates to whatever *future* decisions I make that might lead me too close to Satan's snares and make me vulnerable to his attacks. So these three requests cover the past, the present, and the future, and each of our prayer needs can be put into one of these categories.

FASTING

In the Sermon on the Mount, after Jesus completed His instructions about prayer, He gave a brief word about fasting (Matthew 6:16–18).

Fasting isn't something we do either to impress people or to earn something from God. True fasting grows out of an inner concern—a burden so great that we set aside the normal activities of life and concentrate wholly on the spiritual purpose at hand.

Jesus made it clear that fasting must be voluntary and

come from the heart; it must be sincere; and unless others are fasting together with us, it must be a private exercise between the believer and God. If we gain the applause of others, we lose the blessing of God, and it isn't worth it.

One reason true fasting is effective is that there's a subtle but dynamic relationship between the physical and the spiritual. When the body is disciplined, as during fasting, the Holy Spirit has the freedom to clarify the mind and purify the intentions and make our praying and meditating much more powerful. He can use times of fasting and prayer to sanctify our lives and glorify the Lord.

CONCLUSION

There are only three spiritual temperatures in the Christian life: Our hearts are cold or lukewarm or burning. Worship is both the thermometer and the thermostat of the Christian life. If my heart is cold or lukewarm, it will show up in the way I worship God; my worship will be routine, and I'll be in a hurry to get through my Bible reading and praying and be on my way. If my heart is warm toward God, there won't be time enough to meditate on His Word and tell Him all that's on my heart.

If I want to raise my spiritual temperature, the place to start is with my worship.

STUDY QUESTIONS

1. How would you rate your spiritual temperature: cold, warm, or hot?

2. Of the spiritual disciplines mentioned, which ones are evident in your life? Might this have something to do with your spiritual temperature?

3. We don't hear much on fasting these days. Have you ever fasted? Consider fasting for a day sometime (if your health will allow). Use the time you would be eating to pray and meditate. After you've done this a few times, reevaluate your spiritual temperature. It might take some time to get hotter, but that's where discipline comes in.

Chapter 10

My Heart, Christ's Home

By Robert Munger

Be of good courage, and He shall strengthen
your heart, all you who hope in the LORD.

PSALM 31:24

Many years ago I heard a story that has forever left its grip on me—a story about turning over one's life to Christ, letting Him have complete control. Here is the story as retold by a friend of mine:

One evening I invited Jesus Christ into my heart. What an entrance He made! It was not a spectacular emotional thing, but very real. It was at the very center of my life. He came into the darkness of my heart and turned on the light. He built a fire on the hearth and banished the chill. He started music where there had been stillness, and He filled the emptiness with His own loving, wonderful fellowship. I have never regretted opening the door to Christ and I never will.

In the joy of this newfound relationship, I said to Jesus Christ, "Lord, I want this heart of mine to be Yours. I want

You to settle down here and be perfectly at home. Everything I have belongs to You. Let me show You around."

THE LIBRARY

The first room was the study—the library. In my home this room of the mind is a very small room with very thick walls, but it is a very important room. *In a sense, it is the control room of the house.* He entered with me and looked around at the books in the bookcases, the magazines on the table, the pictures on the wall. As I followed His gaze I became uncomfortable.

Strangely, I had not felt self-conscious about this before, but now that He was there looking at these things, I was embarrassed. Some books were there that His eyes were too pure to behold. There was a lot of trash and literature on the table that a Christian had no business reading, and as for the pictures on the wall—the imaginations and thoughts of the mind—some of them were shameful.

I turned to Him and said, "Master, I know that this room needs some radical alterations. Will You help me make it what it ought to be, and bring every thought into captivity to You?"

"Certainly," He said. "First of all, take all the things that you are reading and looking at which are not helpful, pure, good, and true, and throw them out. Now put on the empty shelves the books of the Bible. Fill the library with Scripture and 'meditate therein day and night' (Joshua 1:8). As for the pictures on the wall, you will have difficulty controlling these images, but there is an aid." He gave me a full-sized portrait of Himself. "Hang this centrally," He said, "on the wall of the mind."

I did so, and I have discovered through the years that

when my attention is centered upon Christ Himself, His purity and power cause impure imaginings to retreat. So He has helped me to bring my thoughts into captivity.

THE DINING ROOM

From the study we went into the dining room, the room of appetites and desires. I spent a good deal of time here and put forth much effort in satisfying my wants. I said to Him, "This is a very big room, and I am quite sure You will be pleased with what we serve."

He seated Himself at the table with me and asked, "What is on the menu for dinner?"

"Well," I said, "my favorite dishes: old bones, corn husks, sour garbage, leeks, onions, and garlic right out of Egypt." These were the things I liked—worldly fare.

When the food was placed before Him, He said nothing, but I observed that He did not eat it. I said to Him, "Master, You don't care for this food? What is the trouble?"

He answered, "I have meat to eat that you know not of.… If you want food that really satisfies, seek the will of the Father, not your own pleasures, not your own desires, not your own satisfaction. Seek to please Me. That food will satisfy you." There at the table He gave me a taste of the joy of doing God's will. What a flavor! What nourishment and vitality it gives the soul! There is no food like it in all the world. It alone satisfies.

THE DRAWING ROOM

From the dining room, we walked into the drawing room. This room was intimate and comfortable. I liked it. It had a fireplace, upholstered chairs, a sofa, and a quiet atmosphere. He said, "This is indeed a delightful room. Let us come here often. It is secluded and quiet, and we can have fellowship together."

Well, as a young Christian I was thrilled. I could not think of anything I would rather do than have a few minutes apart with Christ in intimate fellowship.

He promised, "I will be here early every morning. Meet Me here, and we will start the day together."

Morning after morning I would come downstairs to the drawing room, or "withdrawing room" as I liked to think of it. He would take a book of the Bible from the case. We would open it and read together. He would tell me of its richness and unfold to me its truths. My heart warmed as He revealed the love and the grace He had toward me. These were wonderful hours.

Little by little, under the pressure of my many responsibilities, the time began to be shortened. Why, I don't know, but I thought I was too busy to spend time with Christ. This was not intentional, you understand. It just happened that way. Finally, not only was the time shortened, but I began to miss a day now and then. Perhaps it was some other pressing need. I would miss our time together two days in a row and oftentimes more.

I remember one morning when I was rushing downstairs, eager to be on my way, that I passed the drawing room and noticed that the door was ajar. Looking in, I saw a fire in the fireplace and the Master sitting there next to it. Suddenly, in dismay I thought to myself, *He is my guest. I invited Him into my heart! He has come, and yet I am neglecting Him.*

With downcast glance, I said, "Blessed Master, forgive me. Have You been here all these mornings?"

"Yes," He said. "I told you I would be here every morning to meet with you. Remember, I love you. I have redeemed you at great cost. I desire your fellowship. Even if you cannot keep the quiet time for your own sake, do it for Mine."

The truth that Christ desires my companionship, that He wants me to be with Him and waits for me, has done more to transform my quiet time with God than any other single factor. Don't let Christ wait alone in the drawing room of your heart, but every day find time when, with your Bible and in prayer, you may have fellowship with Him.

THE WORKSHOP

Before long, He asked, "Do you have a workshop in your home?" Down in the basement of my heart I had a bench and some equipment, but I was not doing much with it. Once in a while I would go down and fuss around with a few little gadgets, but I wasn't producing anything substantial.

I led Him down there. He looked over to the workbench and said, "Well, this is quite well furnished. What are you producing with your life for the kingdom of God?" He looked at one or two little toys that I had thrown together on the bench. He held one up to me and said, "Are these little toys all that you are producing in your Christian life?"

"Well," I said, "Lord, I know it isn't much and I really want to do more, but after all, I don't seem to have strength or skill to do more."

"Would you like to do better?" He asked. "Certainly," I replied.

"All right. Let Me have your hands. Now relax in Me and let My Spirit work through you." Stepping around behind me and putting His great, strong hands under mine, holding the tools in His skilled fingers, He began to work through me. The more I relaxed and trusted Him, the more He was able to do with my life.

THE PLAYROOM

He asked me if I had a playroom. I was hoping He would not ask about this. There were certain associations and friendships, activities and amusements, that I wanted to keep for myself. One evening when I was leaving to join some college companions, He stopped me with a glance and asked, "Are you going out this evening?"

I replied, "Yes."

"Good," He said. "I would like to go with you."

"Oh," I answered rather awkwardly, "I don't think, Lord Jesus, that You would really want to go with me. Let's go out tomorrow night. Tomorrow night we will go to prayer meeting, but tonight I have another appointment."

"I'm sorry," He said. "I thought that when I came into your home, we were going to do everything together, to be partners. I want you to know that I am willing to go with you."

"Well," I mumbled, slipping out the door, "we will go someplace tomorrow night."

That evening I spent some miserable hours. I felt wretched. What kind of friend was I to Christ when I was deliberately leaving Him out of my associations, doing things and going places that I knew very well He would not enjoy?

When I returned that evening, there was a light on in His room, and I went up to talk it over with Him. I said, "Lord, I have learned my lesson. I cannot have a good time without You. We will do everything together." Then He went down into the playroom of the house and He transformed it. He brought new friends into my life, new satisfactions, lasting joys. Laughter and music have been ringing through the house ever since.

THE CUPBOARD

One day I found Him waiting for me at the door. There was an arresting look in His eye, and He said to me as I entered, "There is a peculiar odor in the house. Something is dead around here. It's upstairs." As soon as He said the words, I knew what He was talking about.

There was a small hall cupboard up there on the landing, just a few feet square. In that cupboard, behind lock and key, I had one or two little personal things that I did not want Christ to see. I knew they were dead and rotting things, but I so wanted them for myself that I was afraid to admit they were there.

I went up with Him, and as we mounted the stairs the odor became stronger and stronger. He pointed to the door. I was angry. That's the only way I can put it. I had given Him access to the library, the dining room, the drawing room, the workshop, and the playroom, and now He was asking me about a little two-by-four cupboard. I said inwardly, *This is too much. I am not going to give Him the key.*

Reading my thoughts, He said, "If you think I'm going to stay with this odor, you are mistaken. I will go out on the porch."

I saw Him start down the stairs. My resistance collapsed. When one comes to know and love Christ, the worst thing that can happen is to sense His companionship withdrawing. I had to surrender.

"I'll give You the key," I said sadly, "but You will have to open up the cupboard and clean it out. I haven't the strength to do it."

With trembling fingers, I passed the key to Him. He took it, walked over to the door, opened it, took out all the putre-fying stuff that was rotting there, and threw it away. Then He cleaned and painted it. It was done in a moment. Oh, what victory and release to have those dead things out of my life!

Things are different since Jesus has settled down and has made His home in my heart.

STUDY QUESTIONS

1. Are there one or more areas in your life where you haven't let Christ be the Master? What are they?

2. Why is it that you hold on to these things? Are these reasons valid in the eyes of God?

3. Take a moment to repent and ask God to take control of these areas of your life. That's the first step.

Adapted from *My Heart, Christ's Home,* by Robert Boyd Munger. Copyright © 1986 InterVarsity Christian Fellowship/USA—revised edition. Used by permission of InterVarsity Press, P.O. Box 1400, Downers Grove, IL 60515. www.ivpress.com.

SECTION TWO

Temptation

The really important thing in life is not
the avoidance of mistakes, but the obedience of faith.
By obedience, the man is led step by step to correct
his errors, whereas nothing will ever happen to him
if he doesn't get going.

PAUL TOURNIER

If you don't surrender to Christ, you surrender to chaos.

E. STANLEY JONES

No pain, no palm; no thorns, no throne;
no gall, no glory; no cross, no crown.

WILLIAM PENN

Obey...take up your cross...deny yourself....
It all sounds very hard. It is hard.
Anyone who tells you differently is peddling
spiritual soothing syrup, not real Christianity.
And yet, in a strangely paradoxical way, it is also easy.
With every cross that we lift in obedience to
Christ comes the strength to carry it.
It is always a package deal.

LOUIS CASSELS

The Truth About
Temptation

BY BRUCE WILKINSON

To take all that we are and have and hand it
over to God may not be easy; but it can be done.

PAUL E. SCHERER

*D*o you know what lies right between you and your next sin? Something called a "temptation." Therefore, the moment you become serious about personal holiness is the moment you must also become serious about times of temptation. Now that you have been introduced to the subject of biblical holiness, it is time for you to be introduced to the subject of temptations: what they are and how they work.

Temptations are strategic in your quest for personal holiness. Why? As we said at the beginning of this book, temptations lie between you and your goal of holiness. How? Temptations are the entry door to every sin. Even though you might not have recognized it, you were tempted before you sinned.

Let's suppose your best friend at work has a problem. He's a compulsive shoplifter. He's already been caught twice and booked once. You've never understood it, but today you are at the mall together looking for a birthday present for his wife.

You've been talking back and forth and then you notice that he's sweating. It's the dead of winter, and it must be only sixty-eight degrees in the store. So you ask him what's the matter. He looks down at the floor and admits that every moment he has severe temptation to steal. He admits that every second is a desperate struggle not to steal everything in sight. And if he doesn't get out of there in five minutes, he's going to be in real trouble.

What happened? You both saw the same things. Nothing tempted you and everything tempted him.

But then everything changes. Three weeks later you're together on a business conference halfway across the country, far away from home. That night in your room, you're the one sweating. You promised yourself you wouldn't turn on those X-rated movies again. But you can't go to sleep. It's two in the morning and neither your cold shower or your sleeping pills worked. Your shoplifter friend is in the next room sound asleep and never even gave the TV a second thought—and here you are with your hand trembling as it moves closer and closer to the remote control. You haven't given in yet, but the temptation is just too great.

What's behind these temptations? Why do some things wield so much control over you while other things seem powerless?

Here's What the Bible Teaches

The Bible reveals more secrets than any other book ever written. It peels away the covers and puts everything into the light for all to see. Do you know what it reveals about your temptations? James 1:14 says it clearly: "But each one is tempted when he is drawn away by his own desires and enticed."

What was the real cause of those severe temptations? Was it those department store products for your friend or those X-rated movies for you? It may appear so, but it really isn't. Not even for a moment.

The temptation is nothing on the outside, but everything on the inside. Look how the Bible reveals the real source: "when he is drawn away by his own desires." The source of temptation is inside you! A temptation can be a true temptation only if it tempts you. If it doesn't tempt you, then it's just another department store product or television set in some distant hotel room.

The word *desires* is the word we translate *lusts* and appears in the following verses, which help clarify quickly what really is the root of all temptation.

> Where do wars and fights come from among you? Do they not come from your desires for pleasure that war in your members? You lust and do not have. (James 4:1–2)

> But put on the Lord Jesus Christ, and make no provision for the flesh, to fulfill its lusts. (Romans 13:14)

> That you put off, concerning your former conduct, the old man which grows corrupt according to the deceitful lusts. (Ephesians 4:22)

> But those who desire to be rich fall into temptation and a snare, and into many foolish and harmful lusts which drown men in destruction and perdition. (1 Timothy 6:9)

Beloved, I beg you as sojourners and pilgrims,
abstain from fleshly lusts which war against your
soul. (1 Peter 2:11)

Rational Lies

What a revelation! Since temptations are only temptations
because of that which is inside us, then none of us can
blame "him" or "her" or "it" ever again. The only one we
dare blame for that temptation is what lies in the lust of our
own hearts.

Passing the blame to the thing outside us has always been
the way to squirm out of the responsibility and accountability. Ever heard those famous words, "The woman made me
eat it" or "The woman that You gave me…" or "The fruit
looked so good and I just had to"?

You may have even said something like "God made me
do it" or "The temptation was just too strong; I couldn't help
myself" or "It's not my fault; it's in my family line" or even the
old standby "The devil made me do it."

Sound familiar? They're the normal lies we tell ourselves
when we want to give ourselves permission to sin. We make
the lies so logical in our minds that giving in to the temptation is the only thing to do. These are called "rational lies."

Take It from Paul

The apostle Paul faced temptation time after time, but he
learned a remarkable truth about how to overcome those
temptations. Instead of buying into the lies, he knew that:

No temptation has overtaken you except such as is
common to man; but God is faithful, who will not
allow you to be tempted beyond what you are able, but

with the temptation will also make the way of escape,
that you may be able to bear it. (1 Corinthians 10:13)

How wonderful! God *never* allows *you* to be "tempted
beyond what *you* are able."

But it doesn't stop there! Not only does God never allow
you to be tempted beyond what you are able, but God always
does something else: He Himself makes the way of escape out
of that temptation.

God is always there for you when you are tempted.
Always. Not passively watching, but actively intervening. You
see, the Bible reveals that God *makes* something just for you:
"the way of escape." God not only limits the strength of the
temptation, but He also provides the escape route out of that
temptation.

> The tendency is strong to say, "Oh, God won't be so
> stern as to expect me to give up that!" but He will;
> "He won't expect me to walk in the light so that I
> have nothing to hide," but He will; "He won't expect
> me to draw on His grace for everything," but He will.
> (Oswald Chambers)

Now look closely at that verse. Did you see the magnificent three-letter word? Not "a" way of escape. Not "many"
ways of escape. Just "the" way of escape. You see, the Lord
reveals that He makes *the* way of escape for you at that very
time, in that very situation, just for you. It's *the* way of escape
for *you* during your time of temptation. I don't know about
you, but this rocks me to my boots. To think that God—the
God of the universe—also created for me the way out. There
can be no doubt about it, then, can there? God doesn't want

me to sin, and He Himself has done everything necessary in every temptation to provide for me the escape!

LOOK UP AND GET OUT

So the next time you feel trapped, just look up to find the way out. It will be there every time. Maybe it will be through the high mountain pass, or it will be through the trapdoor, or perhaps through the tunnel dug deep beneath the enemy's attacking forces. How do I know? Because the Bible says, "God is faithful and will make the way of escape."

I'll be honest with you. I've still got dirt under my fingernails from the last tunnel that He dug—just for me. And maybe, just maybe, the following chapters will help you find a way of escape from those lustful desires within.

Chapter 11

Open Manholes and Sudden Sin

By Max Lucado

It is easier to stay out than to get out.
MARK TWAIN

*I*t happens in an instant. One minute you are walking and whistling, the next you are wide-eyed and falling. Satan yanks back the manhole cover, and an innocent afternoon stroll becomes a horror story. Helplessly you tumble, aware of the fall but unable to gain control. You crash at the bottom and stare blankly into the darkness. You inhale the evil stench and sit in Satan's sewage until he spits you out and you land, dumbfounded and shell-shocked, on the sidewalk.

Such is the pattern of sudden sin. Can you relate to it? Very few sins are premeditated and planned. Very few of us would qualify for Satan's strategy team. We spend our time avoiding sin, not planning it. But don't think for one minute that, just because you don't want to fall, you won't. Satan has a special trick for you, and he only pulls it out when you aren't looking.

This yellow-bellied father of lies doesn't dare meet you face-to-face. No sir. Don't expect this demon of demons to challenge you to a duel. Not this snake. He hasn't the integrity to tell you to turn around and put up your dukes. He fights dirty.

He is the master of the trapdoor and the author of weak moments. He waits until your back is turned. He waits until your defense is down. He waits until the bell has rung and you are walking back to your corner. Then he aims his dart at your weakest point and...

Bull's-eye! You lose your temper. You lust. You fall. You take a drag. You buy a drink. You kiss the woman. You follow the crowd. You rationalize. You say yes. You sign your name. You forget who you are. You walk into her room. You look in the window. You break your promise. You buy the magazine. You lie. You covet. You stomp your feet and demand your way.

You deny your Master. It's David disrobing Bathsheba. It's Adam accepting the fruit from Eve. It's Abraham lying about Sarah. It's Peter denying that he ever knew Jesus. It's Noah, drunk and naked in his tent. It's Lot, in bed with his own daughters. It's your worst nightmare. It's sudden. It's sin.

Satan numbs our awareness and short-circuits our self-control. We know what we are doing and yet can't believe that we are doing it. In the fog of weakness, we want to stop but haven't the will to do so. We want to turn around, but our feet won't move. We want to run, and pitifully, we want to stay.

It's the teenager in the backseat. It's the alcoholic buying "just one." It's the boss touching his secretary's hand. The husband walking into the porn shop. The mother losing her temper. The father beating his child. The gambler losing his money. The Christian losing control. And it's Satan gaining a foothold.

Confusion. Guilt. Rationalization. Despair. It all hits. It hits hard. We numbly pick ourselves up and stagger back into our world. "O God, what have I done?" "Should I tell someone?" "I'll never do it again." "My God, can You forgive me?"

No one who is reading these words is free from the treachery of sudden sin. No one is immune to this trick of perdition. This demon of hell can scale the highest monastery wall, penetrate the deepest faith, and desecrate the purest home.

Some of you know exactly what I mean. You could write these words better than I, couldn't you? Some of you, like me, have stumbled so often that the stench of Satan's breath is far from a novelty. You've asked for God's forgiveness so often that you worry that the well of mercy might run dry.

Want to sharpen your defenses a bit? Do you need help in reinforcing your weaponry? Have you tumbled down the manhole one too many times? Then consider the following ideas.

First, *recognize Satan*. Our war is not with flesh and blood but with Satan himself. Do like Jesus did when Satan met Him in the wilderness. Call him by name. Rip off his mask. Denounce his disguise. He appears in the most innocent clothing: a night out with the boys, a good book, a popular movie, a pretty neighbor. But don't let him fool you! When the urge to sin rears its ugly head, look him squarely in the eye and call his bluff. "Get behind me, Satan!" "Not this time, you dog of hell! I've walked your stinking corridors before. Go back to the pit where you belong!" Whatever you do, don't flirt with this fallen angel. He'll thresh you like wheat.

Second, *accept God's forgiveness.* Romans chapter 7 is the emancipation proclamation for those of us who have a tendency to tumble. Look at verse 15: "I do not understand what I do. For what I want to do I do not do, but what I hate I do" (NIV).

Sound familiar? Read on. Verses 18 and 19: "For I have the desire to do what is good, but I cannot carry it out. For what I do is not the good I want to do; no, the evil I do not want to do—this I keep on doing" (NIV).

Man, that fellow has been reading my diary! "What a wretched man I am! Who will rescue me from this body of death?" (v. 24, NIV).

Please, Paul, don't stop there! Is there no oasis in this barrenness of guilt? There is. Thank God and drink deeply as you read verse 25 and verse 1 of chapter 8: "Thanks be to God—through Jesus Christ our Lord!... Therefore, there is now no condemnation for those who are in Christ Jesus" (NIV).

Amen. There it is. You read it right. Underline it if you wish. For those in Christ there is no condemnation. Absolutely none. Claim the promise. Memorize the words. Accept the cleansing. Throw out the guilt. Praise the Lord. And...watch out for open manholes.

STUDY QUESTIONS

1. What's the best way to recognize Satan when you're in the heat of battle with temptation?

2. Can you list several ways to fight Satan once you've recognized him?

3. Falling into sin is the easy part. Avoiding it and asking for forgiveness once you've fallen are much more difficult. Read 1 John 1:9. What is God's promise to those who confess their sins?

Taken from *On the Anvil*, by Max Lucado. Copyright © 1985 by Max Lucado. Published by Tyndale House Publishers. Used by permission.

Chapter 12

The Squeeze

BY TIM STAFFORD

No temptation has overtaken you except such as is common to man;
but God is faithful, who will not allow you to be tempted
beyond what you are able,
but with the temptation will also make a way of escape,
that you may be able to bear it.

1 CORINTHIANS 10:13

Do you know what unhappy secret I find more discouraging than anything else in my life? It's the feeling I get right after I have given in again to temptation—after I go into a self-pitying sulk or look at a dirty magazine.

I have no doubt about forgiveness. I know that God will take away the sin and make me new. But I wonder if I will ever escape temptation. When it comes down to it, do I really have any strength to resist? I can picture myself failing again and again and again.

So I have thought about temptation, wondering if there is a key, a magic secret, to resisting it. "Yielding to God" or "turning to the Lord" are phrases that have helped at times. But I have found there is no magic in phrases. I cannot turn away from temptation just by putting myself through some mental gymnastics.

Religious "techniques" have left me very discouraged. I will think I have the answer. Then, giving in to temptation again, I will abruptly know that I don't.

THE PROBLEM IS…

You can be tempted anywhere, anytime: in church, alone, in the wilderness (where, in fact, Jesus was most severely tempted). So how are you going to "avoid temptation"?

You can't really. Some people try to lock temptation out of their lives. They go only to "safe" parties and "safe" movies, and they have "safe" friends. They stay away from the beach and from non-Christian books. They build up a set of rules for themselves to follow rigidly so that temptation will never find a crack in their personalities. All these things may be appropriate at times in keeping the door to temptation closed. But any real solution has to deal with the brain as well. If you are free from temptation in your own thoughts, you can conquer the problems that friends and things bring into your life.

GETTING IN DEEP

I find an analogy helpful. Real, physical pressure is a lot like the pressure of temptation. You can "escape" it only to a point. Do you think a submarine, since it's watertight, can go down as deep as it likes? It cannot. Even the atomic submarines built strongly enough to batter through the ice at the North Pole have a maximum depth. A submarine known as *Thresher* exceeded that depth some years ago. When the pressure became too great, the seawater crushed the sub's heavy steel bulkheads as if it were a plastic model. Searchers found only little pieces of that huge submarine. The tremendous weight of the sea had smashed its strong steel hull. That is pressure.

What if you want to go deeper, though, to reach the bottom of the sea? There are crafts built specially for that. They are strictly for research—steel balls lowered into the ocean on a cable. One researcher can just fit inside, shielded by the heavy steel armor. As he descends, he peers out through a thick glass plate, looking into the depths of the ocean to see what life may survive under such pressure.

He sees fish. You might expect these fish, living at such depth, to be built along the lines of an army tank. They are not. Where the little submarine has inches of steel to protect it, these fish have normal skin, a fraction of an inch thick. They swim freely and curiously about the craft. They sometimes flash neon lights. They have huge eyes. They are as exotic as any fish you will ever see. How can they survive under such pressure? They have a secret: equal and opposite pressure inside themselves.

THE ARMOR OF GOD

In real life, some Christians deal with pressure by putting on inches of steel plate. They shield themselves from the outside world and strap themselves into a narrow space, peering out into the darkness. They are safe inside. But God's kind of freedom is more like the fish's. We keep our shape not through steel plate, but by God's Spirit, who gives us inside strength to deal with each pressure point in our lives.

Romans 12:2, a noted passage of the Bible, essentially says this: "Don't be squeezed into the mold of this world, but be transformed by the renewing of your mind." Pressure from the outside wants to make you conform—to be just like everyone else. The Spirit of God counteracts that from the inside, through your mind.

FUN—FOR A WHILE

It's no use telling yourself temptation doesn't exist. If you are on a diet, a piece of blueberry pie looks appealing, and there is nothing evil about that. I have heard people say that sin is really no fun, but that is not true. Sin is fun…for a while.

What makes temptation not fun in the long run are the things that come with it. You may enjoy a piece of pie today, but that means tomorrow you won't enjoy standing on the scales. You may enjoy self-pity today, but too many days of it will mean self-pity becomes *all* you will get to enjoy since you won't have any friends. Premarital sex may be enjoyable today, but what kind of attitudes and relationships are you building for tomorrow?

To change your mind so it will have the strength to resist temptation, you need to appeal to higher loyalties, stronger desires. Resisting temptation is basically simple, if you think of it. It's a choice. You can look over the options and decide what you want to do. The problem is that temptation's pleasures are often more obvious and immediate than the pleasures of not giving in. Besides, your mind has been twisted again so you cannot always see clearly what is really good for you. It *does* seem better to be loved by your crowd of friends than to be loved by God. So you need to renew your mind— get in touch with what's really best for you. You need to retrain your mind so that those rewards become as obvious as the rewards you get for giving in to temptation. Perhaps these principles will help that process.

1. *Know what you're getting into.* Think about the long-term results of how you act. Today, it may be easier to fight with your fiancée and get your own way. But what kind of relationship are you building for the future? On the other hand, what will obeying God lead to? If you can see the

attraction of the kind of life God wants to plant in you, you will be less tempted to choose some other short-term pleasure. The Bible is full of commentary on how good God's life is. Many of the Psalms speak of the sheer enjoyment of being in touch with God, obedient to Him, relishing the joys of His world. Some of the Psalms also frankly confront the bitter feelings that come when you see unbelievers happy and successful without God, while your godliness seems unrewarded. Read those psalms and work on appreciating the advantages of not giving in to temptation.

2. *Replace tempting thoughts with something better.* You can't ignore temptation, but you can fill your thoughts with something else. Often prayer helps—and not necessarily prayer for help in resisting temptation. I often begin praying for friends.

Sometimes the best thing you can do is to pick up an interesting book, call up a friend, or start working on a project. If you are tempted to go to an X-rated movie, look for another movie instead. The problem with many temptations is that they are close and immediate. If you can put them off a while and give your mind a chance to recover from its panic, you will be in better shape to see the bigger picture.

Breaking Patterns

3. *Your mind tends to follow patterns. Change the patterns, and you change your mind.* In a family, kids are always fighting over what TV programs to watch. They should change the pattern by figuring out ahead of time what shows they will watch and reach some compromise long before the tube is turned on.

For me, being tired often means getting depressed. I can lecture myself that I have no right to feel so sorry for myself. But a more effective solution is to go to bed when I am tired. Somehow that takes the drama out of resisting temptation. I outflank it instead of pacing the floor and praying for strength to resist it.

4. *Break the pattern of failure by confession.* When you go over your mistakes with another person, it changes your attitude. For one thing, you receive forgiveness, and your mind is put at rest. You don't get down on yourself and repeat your failures because of an I-did-it-once-what-does-one-more-matter? attitude. For another thing, a friend can help you to hold to your decision not to give in to temptation anymore. He or she can check up on you, encourage you, and pray for you.

If, for instance, you have said something unkind about another person, admitting what you did and asking forgiveness from the person you gossiped to makes it far less likely you will ever want to do it again. You have confronted your sin in the open. You will remember that the next time you are tempted.

REMEMBER YOUR IDENTITY

5. *Above all, remember who you are: a child of God, loved by Him.* When tempting thoughts come, recall that fact to your mind: "I could act that way, but does that really bring honor to God? I want to be loyal and loving to Him the way He is to me." The more you understand God's love, the more you will want to be close to Him and obedient to Him. Some of your temptations will simply vanish—they will begin to seem stupid. Their pleasures will be insignificant compared with the good things you are experiencing.

Reinforce this understanding of your own identity by reading the Bible and applying what it says, by talking to God, by talking with friends, by listening to what pastors and other Christians say, and especially by worshiping and thanking God for what He has done for you. Christ's message is this: You simply don't have to act in the old way. You are a new person with a whole new way of acting. As much as God has loved you, how can you reject that love by ignoring what He says?

You get stronger every time you beat temptation. Each success is an exercise building you up. The more you experience what joy God has for you in life, the less appealing that old life seems. There will always be more temptations as long as you live on this earth. But the closer you come to God, the less you will want to disappoint Him.

ONE MORE POINT

Each of us has at least one area of special weakness. We may find temptation too strong there and experience repeated failures. Often we become discouraged and are tempted by a much worse sin: hopelessness.

At these times it is more important than ever to realize the limitless nature of God's forgiveness. It *is* limitless, which is hard for us to understand. But if you cling to it, someday you will understand. Not only that, but someday the area you are weakest in will be transformed into a special strength.

STUDY QUESTIONS

1. What are two ways to "equalize" the pressure of temptation?

2. What patterns do you have in your life that are not pleasing to God? How can you break those sinful patterns?

3. What temptations are you continually experiencing that seem to get the best of you every time? How can you best overcome these obstacles to a closer walk with God?

From *Unhappy Secrets of the Christian Life*, by Philip Yancey and Tim Stafford. Copyright © 1979. Published by Campus Life Books/*Campus Life* magazine.

Chapter 13

To Tell the Truth

By R. C. Sproul

LORD, who may dwell in your sanctuary?
Who may live on your holy hill?
He whose walk is blameless and who does what is righteous,
who speaks the truth from his heart and has no slander on his tongue.

PSALM 15:1–3, NIV

What is the most important virtue of the Christian life? To ask such a question is to plunge into an abyss of almost impossible confusion. All virtue is important, and to attempt to single out the most important of all seems like a fool's errand. We immediately think of Paul's words regarding faith, hope, and love—which the apostle does not shrink from rating in importance when he says, "The greatest of these is love."

When James speaks of the priority of virtue he says, "Above all—swear not by…but let your yea be yea and your nay be nay." Surely for James it was a matter of top priority that the Christian's word be reliable and trustworthy. Behind this concern lies the whole scope of biblical concern for the sanctity of truth. God Himself is the fountain of all truth and

His Word is truth. His incarnate Son is the very incarnation of truth.

The unusual indictment of Scripture against fallen humanity may be seen in the sad conclusion that "all men are liars" (Psalm 116:11). This is a sin endemic to fallen human nature and one that is not instantly cured by regeneration. It is the character trait that clearly distinguishes us from God. God is a covenant keeper; He speaks no falsehood. We are covenant breakers, spreading lies even in our promises.

It is Satan who is called the "father of lies." Sadly, he has sired many children. We are all by nature his offspring in this regard. It was the serpent in Eden who uttered the first lie: "You will not...die.... You will be like God"(Genesis 3:4–5). By that lie the human race was seduced and plunged into corruption. It is no small thing that the ruination of original righteousness was provoked by a lie. It was the lie that was the catalyst for the change from original righteousness to original sin.

The judgment of God upon the liar is given. Revelation 21:8 declares that all liars shall have their part in the lake of fire. It avows that the destiny of the liar is hell. If this means that everyone who has ever told a lie will end up in hell, then all of us are bound for perdition.

To tell a lie even once makes a person a liar. Since Scripture affirms that all men are liars, it would seem to suggest that all will perish. But this is not the conclusion Scripture reaches. Our lies are covered by the atonement. But this grace is not a license to lie with impunity. The lie means a serious offense against God and our neighbor. To persist in lying is inconsistent with sanctification, and the person who is characterized by the habit of lying is not Christian.

Yet Christians lie and often with great facility. We lie

because we fear the consequences of the truth. We lie to cover up our sins. The lie tends to take on a life of its own, breeding further lies to cover up the first one.

There are other ways we lie besides direct distortions. We lie when we fail to keep our word. When we say we will do something and then don't do it, we lie. When we say we will not do something and then do the very thing we say we would not do, we lie.

This past summer I had to take two trips to the north that were scheduled about ten days apart. I considered simply staying up north for the entire duration rather than coming home in the interim. But to do so would have required my being absent from home on my daughter's thirty-fifth birthday. Now, for a father to miss his daughter's thirty-fifth birthday may not seem as calamitous as missing her eighth or ninth, but my decision to return home was a "no-brainer" for reasons of history. When my daughter was younger I missed several of her birthdays. Each one I missed because I was away for "important" reasons. Each time she said to me, "Daddy, you promised." Daddy did promise and Daddy broke those promises. And Daddy is still haunted by the pain he caused his daughter then.

In the courtroom the witness is "sworn in." He is required to take the oath "to tell the truth, the whole truth, and nothing but the truth" under the penalty of perjury if the oath be broken. This is a strange phenomenon made necessary because we can lie by means of the half-truth. The half-truth is a ploy designed to deceive while technically telling the truth, and thus misleads the hearer. So is the mixed truth that adds the cross of deception to the nugget of truth that is distorted by it.

I can remember running out the door when our phone

rang so that my wife could tell the person calling me that I wasn't "in." It was a contrivance designed to bend the truth and seek refuge in a half-truth that was really a lie.

Relationships are harmed and often destroyed by the lie. We have far more acquaintances than we have close friends. We choose our close friends carefully. We seek friends who share our concerns, our likes and dislikes, etc. But above all, we want close friends we can trust with our very lives. The chronic liar has few friends. Nobody wants to trust his or her life to someone whose word is no good.

Dr. John Gerstner, who once remarked, "I'd rather die than lie," told the story of having a contractor do a small repair job for him. The man said he would arrive at a certain time to do the work. Dr. Gerstner arranged his schedule to be home at the appointed time. The workman failed to show up. That evening Dr. Gerstner called him. The man explained that another job opportunity that was far more lucrative opened up for him. He promised that he would do the job the next day. Dr. Gerstner declined the offer and hired another contractor whose yea meant yea.

This sort of thing occurs regularly. The missed appointment. The pledge that isn't paid. The bill that is not paid on its due date.

Perhaps the worst and most damaging lie we speak is not the lie we say to someone, but the lie we speak about someone. This is the slander and false witness that is forbidden explicitly by the ninth commandment. This is the lie that steals a person's reputation and sullies his or her good name. Slander is the stock and trade of Satan, whose very name means "slanderer." His favorite pastime is to bring false accusations against the people of God.

For the Christian, we must understand that it is far better

to be lied to than to lie, to suffer broken promises to us than to break them, arid to be slandered than to slander. We are to pursue the truth and not give place to falsehood.

STUDY QUESTIONS

1. Why was it a top priority for James that the Christian's word be true?

2. Do you agree with James that it is of utmost importance to "let your yea be yea"? Do you practice this belief in your life?

3. Would you be willing to take the oath "to tell the truth, the whole truth, and nothing but the truth" if you were called as a witness at a trial? Are you willing to take the same oath to be a witness for Christ every day?

Reprinted from the June 1997 issue of *Tabletalk* with permission of Ligonier Ministries, Inc., P.O. Box 547500, Orlando, FL 32854; or call 1-800-435-4343.

Chapter 14

Anger

By Patrick Morley

"I lose my temper, but it's all over in a minute," said the student.
"So is the hydrogen bomb," I replied.
"But think of the damage it produces!"

GEORGE SWEETING

Dan and his wife, Shirley, were driving home from a welcomed night out for dinner. The Baltimore streets were crowded with traffic. As Dan slowed for a traffic light, a cab driver swerved his steed into the narrow space in front of Dan's car.

Dan leaned on the horn and began to yell expletives at the cabbie. But the light turned green, and the driver took off. Dan decided to teach this cabbie a lesson and began to chase him down the street, honking and screaming and waving his hands out the window.

Finally, the cab driver caught a red light, and Dan pulled alongside the passenger door of the cab. He ranted and raved, but the cab's window was rolled up. After thirty seconds or so, the cab driver leaned over, rolled down his window, and dryly asked Dan, "What do you want me to do, buddy—drop dead?"

What is something that really makes you angry? Not long ago I was walking out of the large mall where we shop and saw a man tongue-lashing his seven-year-old son. His timid wife, holding an infant child, looked on, her demure face frozen in apprehension. Suddenly, without warning, the father wound up and slugged his son in the face.

The boy began to cry, the mother became hysterical, and I flushed with the rage of injustice until I thought the veins in my neck would burst. Nothing makes me more angry than to see a father strike his child with a closed fist.

THE PROBLEM

How did you answer the question, "What makes you angry?" I wonder if, like me, you thought of an instance when righteous anger boiled inside you, or if your mind reflected on a time you were angry because you couldn't have your own way.

Occasionally, we become angry for a righteous cause, but 99 percent of the time we become angry because we are selfish and impatient. I gave a self-serving example of my own anger, but I assure you that 99 percent of the illustrations I could have used would not flatter me very much.

Anger resides behind the closed doors of most of our homes. Personally, I have never lost my temper at the office. I would never want my colleagues to think I couldn't control myself. But rarely a week goes by in which the sparks of family life don't provide good tinder for a roaring fire of anger.

We put on a good show at the office and our social gatherings, but how you are behind the closed doors of your own private castle is how you really are. At the end of a long, hard day at the office, when you pull up the drawbridge to your own private castle, your family gets to live with the *real* you.

Anger destroys the quality of our personal lives, our marriages, and our health. Angry words are like irretrievable arrows released from an archer's bow. Once released, traveling through the air toward their target, they cannot be withdrawn, their damage cannot be undone. Like the arrows of the archer, our angry words pierce like a jagged blade, ripping at the heart of their target.

When anger pierces the soul of the home, the lifeblood of the family starts to drain away. You may notice that a secretary seems to find you attractive. You reflect on how your wife no longer appreciates you. It never occurs to you that it may be you, that if that secretary knew the real you—the angry you that lives secretly behind the closed doors of your home—she would find you about as desirable as a flat tire.

This chapter is addressed to the *real you* that lives behind closed doors. That's the man I would like to talk to, and that includes me.

WHAT MAKE US ANGRY THAT SHOULDN'T?

Seven reasons for anger stir up our sinful nature and hamper our effort to live by the Spirit. In a life fully surrendered to the Lordship of Jesus Christ, these seven reasons for anger are opportunities to either become angry, or to trust God with yet another area of our lives.

1. *Violation of rights.* Everyone believes they have certain rights. On a physical level, we each feel we have certain "space" rights. Psychologists tell us we consider an eighteen-inch zone in front of our face as private. One reaction to the invasion of this space is to fester in anger.

We feel we have many other rights: common courtesies, constitutional freedoms, the right to earn a living and to raise a family as we see fit. When our rights are violated, we become angry. Proverbs 19:11 tells us, "A man's wisdom gives him patience, it is to his glory to overlook an offense" (NIV).

2. *Disappointment with station in life.* Many people become bitter with anger when they begin to suspect that their "oyster" doesn't have the pearl they wanted. Many of us need to accept our lot in life as from the Lord, provided we have been faithful with our abilities.

For others, Proverbs 19:3 sets the record straight: "A man's own folly ruins his life, yet his heart rages against the LORD" (NIV). Fewer slots exist at the top than men trying to fill them. If we are not content with what we have, the issue is not getting more but learning to be content with our circumstances.

3. *Blocked goals.* Setting and achieving realistic goals can be a great source of personal satisfaction. Everyone sets goals, though some people are not consciously aware of the process. When we are blocked from achieving our goals, for good cause or not, we frequently respond in anger.

Psalm 37:5–8 gives us the best formula for setting goals and responding when they are blocked:

Commit your way to the LORD; trust in him and he will do this: He will make your righteousness shine like the dawn, the justice of your cause like the noonday sun. Be still before the LORD and wait patiently for him; do not fret when men succeed in their ways, when they carry out their wicked schemes. Refrain from anger and turn from wrath; do not fret—it leads only to evil. (NIV)

4. *Irritations.* Life's little irritations often seem to weigh more heavily on us than our true dilemmas. "She squeezes

the toothpaste from the top, but I squeeze it from the bottom." "Billy! How many times do I have to tell you: Don't bounce that ball in the house!"

Nothing is more irritating to me than a sticky shirt on a hot summer day. You know what I mean, those days you climb into a car that's hot as an oven. Within moments, sweat drips down your face, and your T-shirt is soaked in a couple of minutes. When you arrive at your destination, you climb back out of the car, but your shirt sticks to the back of the car seat.

Ecclesiastes 7:9 urges us, "Do not be quickly provoked in your spirit, for anger resides in the lap of fools" (NIV).

5. *Feeling misunderstood.* Many years ago I heard Dr. Henry Brandt say something which made an indelible impression on me: "Other people don't create your spirit, they only reveal it." When my feelings get hurt, and anger begins its predictable rise within me, I have to confess that the other person isn't making me angry; he or she only reveals the anger that was already there, lurking just below the surface of my conscious thoughts.

We often think people don't understand us: our feelings, our attitudes, our abilities, our potential. They probably don't. But holding a "pity party" and becoming angry doesn't help us resolve the misunderstanding.

Benjamin Franklin commented, "Anger is never without a reason, but seldom with a good one."

6. *Unrealistic expectations.* I expect strangers to let me down. But when my Christian friends let me down, I can become very upset. The problem is that I often set unrealistically high expectations for my friends and family. They would have to be perfect to live up to some of my expectations!

We frequently don't build enough "slack" into what we

expect from our loved ones. But everyone trips—including ourselves—and we need to build some slack into the formula of our expectations. "Get rid of all bitterness, rage and anger, brawling and slander, along with every form of malice. Be kind and compassionate to one another, forgiving each other, just as in Christ God forgave you" (Ephesians 4:31–32, NIV).

7. *Pathological/psychological.* Occasionally a man will have a problem with anger because of an illness or emotional disorder. A man abused as a child has a higher statistical probability of having the same anger problem as his own father.

A man whose frequent and intense eruptions of anger permanently alienate family members, or worse, cause a man to strike family members with a closed hand during his angry outbursts, should seek professional counseling.

Frankly, most of our anger ends up as sin. The seven reasons for anger we've just reviewed have two characteristics in common: *selfishness* and *impatience.* We are happy as a clam when people agree with us, let us have our own way, and give us what we want. But they don't always see it our way, and our selfishness and impatience often lead to angry outbursts. Surely, though, there are times when anger is appropriate.

IS ANGER EVER JUSTIFIED?

What usually makes us angry are things like our mother-in-law calling as the family is sitting down to dinner, an associate who is habitually late, or the subcompact that dives into the space in front of us as we slow down for a red light.

The things that usually don't make us angry, but should, are racial prejudice, abortion, declining moral values, and other injustices.

When we observe a miscarriage of justice against another person, a controlled, focused anger—righteous indignation—can work for a positive result. Anger over injustice, when the stench of prejudice and bigotry rises to our nostrils, consumes righteous men with a passion to correct the evils of which they have taken note. The greatness of our country rests on the bedrock of our hatred of injustice.

Betrayal by a friend when done with malice is fair cause for anger. A secret told in confidence which is betrayed seems reason enough to become angry. Or an untrue rumor which threatens our reputation seems just cause to make our anger burn.

Even so, our focus should be on avoiding anger. "A fool gives full vent to his anger, but a wise man keeps himself under control" (Proverbs 29:11, NIV). We should keep our anger under control and be patient. "Better a patient man than a warrior, a man who controls his temper than one who takes a city" (Proverbs 16:32, NIV).

WHAT HAPPENS WHEN WE BECOME ANGRY?

My eight-year-old son is an ideal young man. However, he has recently been spilling his chocolate milk. One night at dinner he knocked over a full sixteen-ounce glass, which splattered everywhere. In a huff, I stormed into the bedroom like a pouty little child and refused to return to the dinner table.

"A quick-tempered man does foolish things" (Proverbs 14:17, NIV). When we become angry, we run the risk of becoming very foolish. Of course, this most often happens at home, behind closed doors, where the drawbridge to our private castle has been drawn up for the night.

Our anger has its own consequences. "A hot-tempered man must pay the penalty; if you rescue him, you will have to do it again" (Proverbs 19:19, NIV). Our company once had an executive who became angry at the slightest provocation. He had terrorized the secretarial staff, and the other executives hated him.

I continued to forgive and forget, until finally word came back to me about the impact of his anger. It seems that he had alienated most of the leasing brokers in town, upon whom we rely heavily to help lease our buildings. The straw that broke the camel's back came when I learned he was chewing out tenants who were calling in routine maintenance requests.

One morning I asked this executive to my office and said, "Fred, I love you—I really do. But the business portion of our relationship has come to its natural conclusion. You're fired."

A hot-tempered man must pay the penalty. A hot-tempered man who is rescued will have to be rescued again.

HEALTH CONCERNS

Another result of our anger concerns our health. Doctors estimate that over 60 percent of all diseases are caused by emotional stress. Anger causes the adrenal, thyroid, and pituitary glands to release toxins into our bloodstream. Our anger (and our fear) causes heart attacks, strokes, arteriosclerosis, high blood pressure, ulcers, and scores of other killer diseases.

WHEN IS ANGER A SIN?

Usually. Anger usually works its way into sin. "My dear brothers, take note of this: Everyone should be quick to listen, slow to speak and slow to become angry, for man's anger does not bring about the righteous life that God desires" (James 1:19–20, NIV). When we are patient there is peace, but when we are angry we spark the anger of others. Before we know what happened, our remark about the other fellow's ugly tie escalated to questions about our mother's heritage!

The best guideline for anger is found in Ephesians 4:26–27 (NIV): "'In your anger do not sin': Do not let the sun go down while you are still angry, and do not give the devil a foothold." Three bits of wisdom reside in this passage. First, control yourself and don't sin in your anger. Second, never go to bed angry. We should get down on our knees, forgive, and ask forgiveness. Third, when we are angry, our self-control is at risk. The devil may see a crack in the door and find a foothold. Never let the sun go down and remain angry. That's when anger becomes sin.

RESPONDING TO THE ANGER TEMPTATION

Here are some scriptural guidelines on how to respond to the temptation to sin in your anger.

- *Keep control.* "A fool gives full vent to his anger, but a wise man keeps himself under control" (Proverbs 29:11, NIV).
- *Overlook offenses.* "A man's wisdom gives him patience; it is to his glory to overlook an offense" (Proverbs 19:11, NIV).
- *Avoid angry men.* "Do not make friends with a hot-tempered man, do not associate with one easily angered, or you may learn his ways and get yourself ensnared" (Proverbs 22:24–25, NIV).
- *Appease anger.* "A gentle answer turns away wrath, but a harsh word stirs up anger" (Proverbs 15:1, NIV).

CONCLUSION

Men usually become angry out of selfishness and impatience, rather than outrage over injustice toward others. Men become angry when they shouldn't for the seven reasons we described earlier. The only time our anger is justified is when, under control, we constructively respond to an injustice or a betrayal.

Are you an angry man? Have you been kidding yourself that you are a pretty nice guy because around the office everyone loves you? Remember: How you are behind the closed doors of your private castle is how you really are. That's the man, who along with me, should reread this chapter.

If you are an angry man and would like to overcome your sin of anger, isolate the reasons for your anger from the list of seven reasons for anger in the beginning of the chapter. Ask God to reveal the depth of your sin in the area of anger. Ask Him to forgive you for your sin of anger and to change you into an unselfish, patient man.

The next time you feel your blood beginning to boil, ask yourself, "Am I becoming angry for a *selfish* reason? Am I becoming angry because I am *impatient?*" If you are, *delay saying or doing anything.*

Finally, go to those whom you have hurt with your anger and ask their forgiveness. If you have wounded them deeply, they may not respond right away. That's all right. As you change, they will respond to the new you. What could be more exciting than the prospect of restoring your home from a torture chamber to a castle?

STUDY QUESTIONS

1. Read Ephesians 4:26–27. When does anger become sin?

2. What is a pet peeve of yours? Do you think your anger is a proper response?

3. Have you ever "blown up" at your spouse or other family members? Was it the right response? How should you have responded?

Chapter 15

Career Pressures

BY GARY ROSBERG

Work is the greatest thing in the world,
so we should always save some of it for tomorrow.

DON HEROLD

The men reading this book with you work in every job imaginable. They're laborers, salesmen, teachers, and pastors. They may work the farm or the spreadsheets. They're self-employed, looking for employment, or retired from employment. They're physicians who treat us when we're sick, counselors who salve wounded hearts, mechanics who repair broken engines. Some are in their first job and others in their umpteenth.

But one thing we all have in common: We were designed by our heavenly Father to work. We're called to work—that's been true from the beginning of time. Remember the original setup? "Now the LORD God had planted a garden in the east, in Eden; and there he put the man he had formed…. The LORD God took the man and put him in the Garden of Eden to work it and take care of it" (Genesis 2:8, 15, NIV).

We men have been in partnership with God from the start, and He wants us to work in order to provide for our family. Work is good. Work is God's design. Psalm 104:22–23 gives the timeless picture: "The sun rises…. Then man goes out to his work, to his labor until evening" (NIV).

So if work is good and right and necessary, then why do so many men get tripped up and lose the proper perspective of a healthy balance between work and their homes?

Sometimes it's because we don't respond to danger signs.

THE DANGER

Traveling down Interstate 80 recently, I saw flashing lights ahead. Barricades crisscrossed the road, giving ample warning of road construction. As I approached the site, I saw men and women who were working hard under the heat of the summer sun while thousands of cars passed by each day.

Drivers had been warned to slow down and be alert. Nevertheless, some cars were whizzing by too fast, endangering the safety both of workers and of other motorists. Some of the lane-marking cones meant to steer cars away from equipment and the workers had been knocked aside.

All the elements of danger were present: high rates of speed, workers vulnerable to the elements, pressures to get the job done on time, excessive traffic.

Sounds like our careers, doesn't it? We move quickly at high speeds, trying to do more and more with less and less time, money, and manpower. Workers are vulnerable to all sorts of elements: office politics, downsizing, sexual temptation, lack of training, excessive competition. Are there pressures to get the job done on time? Yes, probably like you experienced just yesterday or today. And how about the excessive traffic? If you live and work like I do, you face that one every day. The demands of phone calls, budgets, project deadlines, personality clashes, contradictory goals—you name it. Our work sites need danger signs as much as I-80 does.

Here's the scoop. For most of us, our work in and of itself is not dangerous. But work out of balance is dangerous both to our health and the health of our family.

Of course we need to work. "If anyone does not provide for his relatives, and especially for his immediate family," Paul said, "he has denied the faith and is worse than an unbeliever" (1 Timothy 5:8, NIV). It couldn't be much clearer. If we don't provide for our families, we're in deep weeds. God calls us to provide. It's our role to provide materially for our families.

What does that mean? For some it's a roof over our heads, food, adequate clothing. For others it's Air Jordan sneakers, trips to Disneyland during spring break, designer clothes, the works. This chapter isn't designed to answer the question, "How much provision is enough?" But it is designed to ask you as a man this question: "Are you so stuck on *material* provision that you are failing to give the *emotional* provision your wife and kids need?"

Emotional provision means not only that the lights are on, but also that someone is home. It means that in addition to providing materially, you save enough energy to invest in the personal needs of your family. It means being generous with your time, your affection, your wisdom, your companionship. It doesn't mean you don't work hard. It means you save enough of you to connect heart to heart. The job isn't done when you've brought home a paycheck, no matter how big it is.

BALANCE

God created us to work, but that work must be in balance. Maybe you have it in balance. You're fulfilled in your job, but that isn't the be-all and end-all of your existence. You have a proper perspective, knowing that someone was doing the job before you and someone will pick it up when you leave. You may be quite creative and successful, but your identity isn't defined solely by the marketplace.

Or perhaps you're realizing that this area of life is out of balance. You may be working two jobs to make ends meet. You may be doing yeoman's labor just to provide for your family. Or maybe work is out of balance for you because it's the only place you're fulfilled. You do your job well, and going home brings only the stress of a fragmented family. You find yourself staying at the office a few more hours or nights than ever before, and you sense your family slipping from you.

Or maybe you're squarely in denial. I once saw a T-shirt that said, "Denial. It isn't a river in Egypt." Everyone—from your wife and kids and parents to the family dog—knows your work schedule is out of balance. Everyone, that is, but you. You may have been told, but you haven't listened. You've closed off any input because down deep, you're afraid to hear the truth. And until a crisis hits, you're likely to continue the pattern.

Balance in your work life doesn't mean you don't work extra hours from time to time. We all do that. It doesn't mean you don't "go for it" and be the best you can be in your career. We all want to pursue excellence. What balance means is that you ask yourself the hard questions, and you're willing to listen to those who know and love you.

When you come home night after night so exhausted that you have nothing left for your family, you ask yourself if you're in a destructive pattern. When your kids stop talking to you about school, problems, or fun times, you ask yourself if you may be out of balance. When you've missed the family dinner three nights this week, and can't remember the last time you saw your son play ball, and can't remember the instrument your daughter plays, you ask yourself whether you've crossed the line.

Balance isn't a trap, but a protection—God's protection—so that we win in our homes and cross the finish line with our wives and kids.

These are hard times for men. We're being pulled both ways. On one hand, we're trying to keep in balance so we can succeed as husbands and dads. On the other hand, the marketplace where we're trying to survive is getting more and more competitive. Many companies are downsizing. Many men are losing their jobs, and countless others are anxious about losing theirs. Many who do manage to keep steady work are faced with a smaller paycheck. We're all being asked to do more with less in our businesses, and we feel the crunch. It all adds up to unwanted pressure for men committed to guarding their hearts in the marketplace.

Our families and our culture demand that we find the balance. If we don't, we're going to lose our families. You can always get another job, but replacing your family is something else again.

Our work has its own built-in tension, being designed as it is to meet our own needs as well as the needs of our families, our employers, and our Lord. Maybe you sense these needs pushing at you from all sides, leaving you in a major crunch. If you feel that stress, take a look at these three plumb lines.

First, is your work pleasing to God? Not only the actual work, but the way you work: your motivation, your use of time, your attitudes toward the job. If you believe that what you're doing is pleasing to God, then you're on the right track.

Second, ask yourself, "Is my family consistently getting only the leftovers of my mental and emotional energy because of my excessive work? Am I offering too little emotional provision at home?" We all have episodes of work stress. That isn't the problem. But if there is a pattern to it, we need to take a long, hard look at the impact our work is having on our family.

Third, is your work pushing you into the danger zone regarding your own emotional, mental, and physical health? If so, it would be wise to get a personal checkup to inventory your work patterns and make some adjustments. Analyze how your emotional strength, mental strength, and physical strength are typically expended, and how (and if) you're replenishing yourself in each of those areas.

AN INVESTMENT ANALYSIS

One evening, over a plateful of blackened redfish, my friend Dennis Rainey challenged me to count the cost of my own overburdened schedule. As we were discussing the ministries God had allowed me to be involved in, Dennis put down his fork and said, "Gary, God has given you many arenas of effectiveness for Him: counseling, speaking, writing, and men's ministry—to name a few. You have the potential to enjoy success in any of those areas. But if you aren't careful, you'll spread yourself too thin and become ineffective in your calling—as well as in your home.

"The question you need to ask yourself is not where *can*

you succeed, but where *must* you succeed. Tell me something, Gary. If you put all the energy you put into your ministry in one hand, and the energy and focus you put into your home in the other hand, what would happen if you flip-flopped them? What would happen to your ministry? What would happen to your home?"

Wise questions from a wise man. In fact, I didn't finish my dinner. You see, out of his love for me, he challenged me to strike the balance. My family demands I find the balance. So does yours, friend.

And if the balance is at times lost as you tip one way or the other, let it tip in the direction of home and family rather than career. If you *must* choose between climbing the career ladder or "being there" for your wife and kids, which side do you honestly want to win? Ask yourself: Isn't it better—much better, in heaven's economy—for your job and career to suffer than for your family to suffer?

FORTUNE OR FAMILY?

So how do we win at home? How do we guard our hearts so that we find the balance and stay out of the danger zone?

Let's go back to the Bible. Jesus said, "What good is it for a man to gain the whole world, and yet lose or forfeit his very self?" (Luke 9:25, NIV).

He could just as easily have asked, "What good is it for a man to gain the whole world, and yet lose or forfeit his own family?"

I don't want to sacrifice my family at the altar of the job. I almost did that in 1983 when my daughter left me out of the family picture. She was the only one who managed to get my attention. My pastor, wife, parents, and friends all tried, to no avail. But Sarah's picture changed my life.

Still, it took *two years* to pull away from the excessive work patterns and get back to the place God most wants me to win: in the home. He wants me to provide not only financially, but also (and more importantly) emotionally and spiritually for the needs of my wife and kids. And He wants you to do the same.

WORK IS NOT THE PROBLEM

Work isn't our problem. Our hearts are. And if we are trying to fill some clawing need in our hearts by excessive work, rather than investing in our relationships at home, then we all lose.

We were designed to work, and our work is good and honorable. We need to do our best and to give our employers their money's worth. We need to be wholehearted men in whatever we do, both on the job and at home. That may mean you won't get promoted as fast on the job. It may mean you won't make as much money. It may mean there won't be as many bonuses or perks.

But it will probably also mean that your wife and kids will finish the race with you. And nothing can compare to that!

Guard your heart.

STUDY QUESTIONS

1. Look at Colossians 3:22–24. What perspective do these verses bring to your daily work? In what ways does knowing your primary responsibility to please the Lord Jesus actually increase your work responsibility? How might it also release you from stress and pressure?

2. How does integrity and the quality of your work have a direct bearing on the effectiveness of your witness to outsiders? In what ways can you improve these two areas?

Taken from *Guard Your Heart*, by Gary Rosberg. Copyright © 1994 by Gary Rosberg. Published by Multnomah Books. Used with permission.

Chapter 16

The Strategic Use of Time

By J. Oswald Sanders

There is a time for everything,
and a season for every activity under heaven.

ECCLESIASTES 3:1, NIV

Busy Christian workers are apt to borrow from the world the expression heard so often: "I don't have the time" or "I am too busy." While it is usually uttered in great sincerity, it is frequently untrue, but the inner attitude it betrays can play havoc with the nervous system and consequently with the spiritual life as well. Is it really true that we do not have enough time? Great men and women never give the impression of being too busy but rather appear to be quite at leisure. It is usually the small and inefficient person who gives the impression of great busyness.

In one of the world's great sermons, "Every Man's Life a Plan of God" by Horace Bushnell, an illuminating paragraph occurs:

Every human soul has a complete and perfect plan cherished for it in the heart of God, a Divine biography which it enters into life to live. This life, rightly unfolded, will be a complete and beautiful whole, led on by God and unfolded by His secret nurture as the trees and the flowers by the secret nurture of the world.

This statement enshrines a wonderful and transforming truth which, rightly apprehended, could impart a dignity and significance to the humblest life. It accords with Paul's claim that "we are his workmanship, created in Christ Jesus unto good works, which God hath before ordained that we should walk in them" (Ephesians 2:10, KJV). If this is true, the corollary is that there are enough hours in each day for us to fulfill God's perfect and particular plan for our lives.

CHRIST'S EXAMPLE

Our Lord moved through life with majestic and measured tread, never in a hurry and yet always thronged by demanding crowds, never giving those who sought His help a sense that He had any more important concerns than their particular interests.

What was His secret? Knowing that every man's life is a plan of God, He realized that His life and all the conditions in which it was to be worked out were alike under the perfect control of His Father. Time held no power over Him. On several occasions He asserted that His hour had not yet come, and implicit in this assertion was the consciousness that His Father's plan had been drawn with such meticulous accuracy that every hour was accounted for and adjusted to the overall purpose of His life.

His calendar had been arranged, and His sole concern on earth was to fulfill the work given Him to do in the allotted hours (John 7:6; 12:23, 27; 13:1; 17:1). Nor would He allow His much-loved mother to interfere with His divinely planned timetable (John 2:4). Deep human affection could not be permitted to anticipate His schedule by two days, or His Father's plan would be marred (John 11:6, 9).

Small wonder, then, that at the close of life He could review it with absolute complacency and utter the self-approving words: "I have finished the work which thou gavest me to do" (John 17:4, KJV), no part of it having been marred by undue haste or imperfectly completed through lack of time. He found sufficient time in the twenty-four hours of the day to do the whole will of God. The Lord's corrective word to His disciples, "Are there not twelve hours in the day?" seems to suggest a quiet, steady confidence in His Father's purpose and the resulting courage, even when confronting enemies and danger.

Interruptions could not disturb His peace because they had already been provided for in the Father's planning, and the wrath of enemies would have to await His "hour." Thus He could pursue His work unmoved, knowing it would be "finished." There would be time for all that God meant Him to do, though there might not always be "leisure so much as to eat."

It is easy to stand afar off and admire in our Lord these desirable qualities which so often are lacking in our own lives. But He is to be followed, not only admired, for He left us an example in this as in all else. We have the same Holy Spirit who indwelt Him to help us. Was Christ sent to earth to fulfill His Father's plan? Was it not said anticipatively of Him, "Lo, I come: in the volume of the book it is written of me, I delight to do thy will, O my God" (Psalm 40:7–8, KJV)? Then He says to us: "As the Father hath sent me, even so send I you," and He who sends will enable to fulfill our ministry.

WHAT IS TIME?

Is time the ticking of the clock, the moving of a shadow? Calendar and clock are only mechanical means by which we record our consciousness of time, not time itself. As we commonly use the word it means "duration," or "a stretch of duration in which things happen." But perhaps the most helpful definition of *time* is "duration turned to account."

Dr. John R. Mott viewed time as our lives measured out to us for work, the measure of the capacity of our lives.

Paul counseled the Ephesian believers to "redeem the time," or as Weymouth renders it, "buy up the opportunities," for time is opportunity. Note that time becomes ours by purchase—it has to be redeemed, bought. We exchange it for certain occupations and activities, important or otherwise, and herein lies the importance of a planned life. When we say we don't have time, it may only be that we do not know how to make use of the opportunity time affords us. Time is a God-given stewardship for which we must render account, and our use of it will determine the value of our contribution to our day and generation.

The difference between one man and another lies largely in his use of time.

THREEFOLD PRESCRIPTION

Here are three constructive suggestions which may be of help to those who are seriously seeking to fill their lives with the greatest possible usefulness to God, and yet to do it without undue strain and tension.

1. *Stop leaks.* Let us not consider our day only in terms of hours but in smaller areas of time. If we look after the minutes, the hours will look after themselves. Few men packed more into a lifetime than the late Dr. F. B. Meyer. Like John Wesley, he divided his life into spaces of five minutes and chided himself if one of them passed in idleness. One would expect such a program to create intolerable strain, but not so with Dr. Meyer. According to his biographer: "His calm manner was not the sleep of an inactive mind, it was more like the sleep of a spinning top. He was never in a hurry because he was always in haste." Just a little while before his death he said to a friend, "I think I am an example of what the Lord can do with a man who concentrates on one thing at one time."

Perhaps few of us ordinary mortals can hope to achieve such a degree of concentration as to make every quarter hour carry the full quota of usefulness, but that does not excuse us from attempting it. For example, it is amazing how much reading can be squeezed into fragments of time redeemed from the trash pile. It is vain to wait until we get time to read seriously—we will never get it. We must make time to read by seizing the minutes we have. We should seek to detect unsuspected leakages of time, and with purpose of heart, *plug the leak.*

2. *Study priorities.* Much time which is not actually wasted is spent on things of only secondary importance. A fool has been described as a man who has missed the proportion of things. Some of us have the unfortunate tendency to be so engrossed in the secondary that we have no time left for the primary. We give such undue attention to petty details that matters of major importance are squeezed out. Especially is this so where spiritual things are concerned.

Our Lord Himself indicated that the secret of progressive living was to sacrifice the pearl of inferior value for the pearl of transcendent worth. Are we doing the most important things, or do we, because of the demands they make, procrastinate where they are concerned? Weigh carefully the respective values of the opportunities and responsibilities which claim attention. Omit altogether or give a very minor place to things of little importance. John Wesley used to say, "Never be unemployed; and never be triflingly employed." May I say here that *disciplined recreation and relaxation are not of secondary importance.* Jesus enjoyed ordinary social life and did not consider it a waste of time to attend a wedding feast. We should from time to time see if we have our priorities right.

3. *Start planning.* Without a proper plan we all tend to drift. If our life is a plan of God, there is appropriate work for each hour, and the Lord will guide us as we pray and plan. Dr. John R. Mott used to devote half a day now and again to laying plans for the days ahead, and he considered it time well invested. In the attitude of prayer ask, "How can I best plan today?" Divide it into parts. There are certain obvious obligations and duties, both spiritual and temporal, which naturally demand a place, and adequate time should be allowed for these. Then there are secondary things, which should be carefully pruned to a minimum and fitted in. When two duties pull in different directions, choose that which after prayer and thought seems more important. If a secular claim crowds a spiritual, do not concede the point unless you have good reason for doing so. In most lives there are every day short gaps left in the program which seem too short to fill with anything important, but these gaps must be filled. Allow sufficient time to ensure punctuality, but not too

much. Buy up the spare minutes as eagerly as a miser hoards his money. *Start planning your days.*

FINAL POINTS

To effect a radical change in our use of time will require strength of purpose and a real dependence on the Lord for His enabling.

It is well to recognize that after we have done all in our power, there will still remain a vast area of need. We cannot meet every call of need. If we sincerely before the Lord plan out our day along the lines suggested and carry it out to the best of our ability, we can and must leave it there. We should refuse to get into bondage about what has not been done. Our responsibility is concerned only with the factors which lie within our power to control.

STUDY QUESTIONS

1. God has a plan for the world. Are you using your time in such a way that you cooperate with God's plan, or are you fighting against that plan?

2. What does Paul mean when he tells the Ephesians to "redeem the time"? Are you heeding his words?

3. What steps can you take to better organize your world so that you can use your time more efficiently?

Taken from *A Spiritual Clinic* by J. Oswald Sanders, copyright © 1958.

Chapter 17

Will I Ever Have Enough?

By Ron Blue

*My God shall supply all your needs according
to His riches in glory by Christ Jesus.*

PHILIPPIANS 4:19

At the age of twenty-four, I had every ingredient needed for successes: an MBA degree, my CPA certificate, a well-paying job with the world's largest CPA firm in their New York office, a driving ambition to be a success, and a supportive and very intelligent wife.

For the next eight years, I proved to myself that anyone could succeed by really putting everything into it. By the time I was thirty-two years old, I had achieved every financial and success goal I had set:

- I had moved rapidly up the corporate ladder.
- I had founded the fastest-growing CPA firm in Indiana, and today it has become one of the fifty largest firms in the United States.

- I, along with others, owned two small banks in Indiana.
- I had a lovely wife and three young daughters.
- I had all of the trappings of success: a new home, new car, country club memberships, and the like.

I had also just committed my life to Jesus Christ and had no needs that I was aware of.

It was during the early seventies, and for the first time in the nation's history, Americans began experiencing "tremendous" inflation rates of 4 percent and 5 percent. The prime rate hit an unbelievable high of 10 percent, and then even went to 12 percent. The dollar was taken off the gold standard, and for the first time in recent history, the United States began running a trade deficit.

In the midst of personal affluence, I began to experience the fear that comes from wondering, "Will I ever have enough? Or, if I do have enough now, will it be enough when I retire? And, by the way, how much is enough?" I believe that everyone, rich and poor, asks themselves these underlying questions more frequently than they would like to admit. These questions are constantly in our subconscious, and therefore we all deal with them somehow—on one hand by hoarding our resources, on the other hand by living out the philosophy of "get all the gusto you can—you only go around once."

The Christian, additionally, is confronted with the question, What is the appropriate Christian lifestyle?

Through the midseventies, I dealt with these questions, both personally and as an adviser to a largely wealthy secular clientele. In 1977, my wife and I experienced God's call to leave the businesses I was involved in and join a new ministry in Atlanta, Georgia. For two years, as our family grew to five children, I helped to develop seminar materials in the areas of decision making, time management, faith planning, and problem solving. Also during the late seventies, I traveled to Africa eleven times, assisting a large Christian organization to apply the principles that we were developing.

I observed during all of this that the same financial questions that my former clients and I had been asking were being asked by others as well: missionaries, affluent Africans, poor Africans, full-time Christian workers, successful American executives, pastors, and friends:

- Will I ever have enough?
- Will it continue to be enough?
- How much is enough?

The questions transcended cultures as well as classes.

In 1979, at the encouragement of Dr. Howard Hendricks, I founded an organization called Ronald Blue & Co., which has as its objective to remove the fear and frustration that Christians experience when they deal with money. The need for this type of counsel and advice is, I believe, pervasive. Christian teaching and application go from the extreme of sharing personal income in communal living, to the "name it, claim it" approach. Both are an attempt to reach God in the way we handle our money, when all the time He is reaching out to us with His wisdom, counsel, and principles.

John MacArthur, pastor of Grace Community Church, Panorama City, California, in his series "Mastery of Materialism," said:

Sixteen out of thirty-eight of Christ's parables deal with money; more is said in the New Testament about money than heaven and hell combined; five times more is said about money than prayer; and while there are five hundred plus verses on both prayer and faith, there are over two thousand verses dealing with money and possessions.

Obviously, the Bible has much to say about money management.

THE FOUR BIBLICAL PRINCIPLES OF MONEY MANAGEMENT

Even though the Parable of the Talents found in Matthew 25:14–30 deals primarily with Christ's return, it has shown me four basic biblical principles of money management that really summarize much of what the Bible has to say regarding money and money management.

1. God owns it all.

"For the kingdom of heaven is like a man traveling to a far country, who called his own servants and delivered his goods to them." (Matthew 25:14)

Very few Christians would argue with the principle that God owns it all, and yet if we follow that principle to its natural conclusion, there are three revolutionary implications. First of all, God has the right to whatever He wants whenever He wants it. It is all His, because an owner has rights, and I, as a steward, have only responsibilities.

When my oldest child reached driving age, she was very eager to use my car and, as her father, I entrusted my car to her. There was never any question that I could take back my car at any time for any reason. She had only responsibilities while I maintained all the rights. In the same way, every single possession that I have comes from someone else: God. I literally possess much but own nothing.

If you own your own home, take a walk around your property to get a feel for the reality of this principle. Reflect on how long that dirt has been there and how long it will continue to be there; then ask yourself if you really own it or whether you merely possess it. You may have the title to it, but that title reflects your right to possess it temporarily, not forever. Only God literally owns it forever.

If I really believe that God owns it all, then when I lose any possession, for whatever reason, emotions may cry out, but my mind and spirit have not the slightest question as to the right of God to take whatever He wants whenever He wants it. Really believing this also frees me to give generously of God's resources to God's purposes and His people. All that I have belongs to Him.

The second implication of God's owning it all is that not only is my giving decision a spiritual decision, but every spending decision is a spiritual decision. There is nothing more spiritual than buying a car, taking a vacation, buying food, paying off debt, paying taxes, and so on. These are all uses of His resources. He owns all that I have.

Think about the freedom of knowing that if God owns it all—and He does—He must have some thoughts about how He wants me to use His property. The Bible reveals many specific guidelines as to how the Owner wants His property used. As a steward, I have a great deal of latitude, but I am still responsible to the Owner. Someday I will give an accounting of how I used His property.

The third implication of the truth that God owns it all is that you can't fake stewardship. Your checkbook reveals all that you really believe about stewardship. A life story could be written from a checkbook. It reflects your goals, priorities, convictions, relationships, and even the use of your time. A person who has been a Christian for even a short while can fake prayer, Bible study, evangelism, and going to church, but he can't fake what his checkbook reveals. Maybe that is why so many of us are so secretive about our personal finances.

2. *We are in a growth process.*

> "His lord said to him, 'Well done, good and faithful servant; you were faithful over a few things, I will make you ruler over many things. Enter into the joy of your lord.'" (Matthew 25:21)

In reading the Scriptures, knowing that our time on earth is temporary and is to be used by our Lord as a training time is inescapable. The whole parable emphasizes this. I would observe that God uses money and material possessions in your earthly life during this growth process as a tool, a test, and a testimony. As Paul said in Philippians 4:11–12:

> Not that I speak in regard to need, for I have learned in whatever state I am, to be content: I know how to be abased, and I know how to abound. Everywhere and in all things I have learned both to be full and to be hungry, both to abound and to suffer need.

Money and material possessions are a very effective tool that God uses to grow you up. Therefore, you need always to ask, "God, what do You want me to learn?" Not "God, why are You doing this to me?" My role as a counselor is to help people discover what God would have them learn, either from the situation of their abundance, or from the situation of their apparent lack of financial resources. God is not trying to frustrate us. He is trying to get our attention, and money is a great attention-getter.

Money is not only a tool, but also a test.

> Therefore if you have not been faithful in the unrigh-
> teous mammon, who will commit to your trust the
> true riches? And if you have not been faithful in what
> is another man's, who will give you what is your
> own? (Luke 16:11–12)

I don't understand it, but I do know that somehow my eternal position and reward is determined irrevocably by my faithfulness in handling property that has been entrusted to me by God.

We are called to be salt and light, as Jesus points out in Matthew 5:13–16. I believe we can say that God can use my use of His resources as a testimony to the world. My attitude as a Christian toward wealth becomes the testimony.

3. The amount is not important.

> "His lord said to him, 'Well done, good and faithful
> servant; you have been faithful over a few things, I
> will make you ruler over many things. Enter into the
> joy of your lord.'" (Matthew 25:23)

When you look back to verse 21 and compare it word for word with verse 23, you will see that the same words were spoken to the slave with five talents and the one with two talents. Both were reminded that they had been faithful with a few things, and both were promised something in heaven. You can draw the conclusion that the amount you have is unimportant, but how you handle what you have been entrusted with is very important.

There is much controversy today about whether an American Christian is more spiritual on one hand by accumulating much or on the other hand by giving it all away. I believe that both are extremes and not reflective of what God says. He never condemns wealth and commends poverty, or vice versa. The principle found in Scripture is that He owns it all. Therefore, whatever He chooses to entrust you with, hold with an open hand, allowing Him to entrust you with more if He so chooses, or allowing Him to take whatever He wants. It is all His. That is the attitude He wants you to develop. And whatever you have, little or much, your attitude should remain the same.

4. *Faith requires action*.

"Then he who had received the one talent came and said, 'Lord, I knew you to be a hard man, reaping where you have not sown, and gathering where you have not scattered seed. And I was afraid, and went and hid your talent in the ground. Look, there you have what is yours.' But his lord answered and said to him, 'You wicked and lazy servant, you knew that I reap where I have not sown, and gather where I have not scattered seed. So you ought to have deposited my money with the bankers, and at my coming I would have received back my own with interest. Therefore take the talent from him, and give it to him who has ten talents. For to everyone who has, more will be given, and he will have abundance; but from him who does not have, even what he has will be taken away. And cast the unprofitable servant into the outer darkness. There will be weeping and gnashing of teeth.'" (Matthew 25:24–30)

The wicked slave knew, but he did nothing. Many of us know what we ought to do, but we disobey or delay. We have emotional faith and/or intellectual faith, but not volitional faith. We know but...

We may know deep down what God would have us do, but we are so bombarded with worldly input which seems to be acceptable that we are paralyzed. We take no action because of the fear of making a mistake biblically or financially. Or we are frustrated and confused. We do only what we feel good about. Living by our feelings rather than "the truth" (John 14:6) can be very dangerous.

STUDY QUESTIONS

1. What are your answers to these three questions: Will I ever have enough? Will it continue to be enough? How much is enough?

2. Do you honestly believe that God owns everything you possess? Do you believe it enough to let it affect the way you use your money?

3. Is your money a tool you use to get what you want out of life—or is it a tool you use to further the kingdom of God?

Reprinted by permission of Thomas Nelson Publishers from the book *Master Your Money*, Copyright © 1991 by Ron Blue.

Chapter 18

Discipline:
Achieving Success Through
Delaying Gratification

BY BILL HYBELS

No horse gets anywhere until he is harnessed.
No steam or gas ever drives anything until it is confined.
No Niagara is ever turned into light and power until it is tunneled.
No life ever grows great until it is focused, dedicated, disciplined.

HARRY EMERSON FOSDIC

$\mathcal{S}$ ome people seem to succeed at everything they try. They have successful careers; they relate well to their families; they may be involved in church and community activities; they are active, growing Christians— they are even physically fit. When you get close to people like this and try to determine just how they manage to fulfill so much of their potential, you find that in almost every case one quality plays a significant role: *discipline.*

By contrast, other people have an embarrassing string of setbacks, disasters, and failures. If you get close to them, and if they are honest with themselves and with you, they will probably offer you a candid appraisal of why these calamities have befallen them. "Well, you know, I just started to let things slide," they may say. "I put off doing my homework." "I neglected to follow up leads." "I didn't push my chair back from the bar." "I didn't take care of myself." "I didn't spend time with my family." "I thought problems would solve themselves." The list of reasons for failure could go on and on, but most of them stem from one conspicuous lack: *discipline*.

Discipline is one of the most important character qualities a person can possess. It plays a key role in developing every area of life. But how many highly disciplined people do you know? Can you quickly think of five people that are truly disciplined in all areas of their lives? Are you disciplined yourself? God has given me hundreds of acquaintances, and only a small fraction of them demonstrate discipline to a significant degree. Not that people do not want to be disciplined—they do. But discipline, I fear, is an endangered character quality.

In various polls, I have asked people what character quality they would most like to have more of. Usually one of the top responses is "discipline." But there is a great deal of confusion as to what discipline really is and how to practice it. People do not know how to develop greater levels of discipline and put it to work for them in everyday life.

What, then, is this thing we don't understand but want more of? I can give you a two-word explanation of this confusing character quality that defines it, captures its essence, and uncovers what is really at its core. These two words are easily remembered. You can think about them during the day and use them in your conversation. Discipline is *delayed gratification*.

First, the Bad News

According to Scott Peck in his book *The Road Less Traveled*, "Delaying gratification is a process of scheduling the pain and pleasure of life in such a way as to enhance the pleasure by meeting and experiencing the pain first and getting it over with." He adds, "It is the only decent way to live." I couldn't agree more.

It takes continual parental prompting over a period of years before most children learn to use this principle, but those who mature properly eventually learn that they will not enjoy dinner and after-dinner activities if they have homework hanging over their heads or if they know the dog needs a bath. That is why well-disciplined students attack their responsibilities—their schoolwork and chores—as soon as possible after school. Once these tasks are finished, they can enjoy the rest of the evening.

As people move out of adolescence into adulthood and the job market, they usually knowingly and of necessity enter the workforce near the bottom rung of the ladder. They willingly put up with long hours, short vacations, repetitive tasks, and minimal pay because they know that, if they endure the entry-level discomfort for a while, the payoff will eventually come in the form of more flexible hours, higher pay, longer vacations, more responsibility, more interesting tasks. They are practicing delayed gratification, purposefully scheduling the pain early, trusting that a much more enjoyable phase will result. This principle, which works well in the job market, can be applied to many other situations as well.

For example, delayed gratification is important to spiritual life. As a pastor, I have often heard people say, "I've learned something over the years. If I discipline myself to spend ten or fifteen minutes early in the morning in a quiet place getting a proper perspective on my walk with the Lord—writing down some thoughts, reading my Bible, listening to a tape, praying—the whole rest of my day seems much more satisfying." Listen closely to what these people are saying: If I roll out of the sack while the house is still cold and invest any time and energy on something worthwhile, then the rest of the day will be better. This is delayed gratification as it pertains to the spiritual walk.

Delayed Gratification in the Family

Discipline also pertains to the relational life. Married couples who understand the value of discipline say to each other early in their relationship, "Let's work very hard on this marriage right now. Let's face all our conflicts as they arise. Let's not let things slide. Let's do whatever it takes right now to make our marriage mutually satisfying." This may require a lot of hard work, and it may be uncomfortable or even painful at times, but it brings wonderful results in the form of more fulfilling and satisfying days ahead.

Discipline is not hard to understand, then, if you can remember the words *delayed gratification*. But understanding discipline and practicing it are two different things. The key to practicing discipline can be described in three words: *advance decision making*. Here's what I mean.

Advance Decision Making

Once you make up your mind that the only decent way to live is to schedule the pain and the tough challenges first so that you can enjoy the pleasure, the rewards, and the payoff later, then you have to take an important practical step. You must make advance decisions as to how you are going to practice discipline in the various dimensions of your life.

For instance, Lynne and I put our family budget together at the beginning of each year. We pray about it, we agree on it, and we put it down on paper. Then we covenant together—that is, we make an advance decision—to abide by our budget, come what may.

Payday comes, and what happens? "I saw the most wonderful lamp. It has our name written on it. And it's on sale." We start smiling at each other. "It would look perfect on that little table, and it would make the room so much brighter. We really need it." Without an advance decision about our budget, we would probably run out and buy that lamp right then. But because we have agreed to live by our budget, we look at the figures and ask, "Is it in there, or isn't it?" If it isn't, that's too bad. The decision has already been made. We don't fight about it or try to backtrack. We live by it.

SPIRITUAL DECISIONS

Most important of all, advance decision making is an important factor in our relationship with God. We know we are saved by grace and not by hard work or planning or discipline. Our spiritual life is God's gift to us, just as our physical life was given to us with no effort on our part. But without practicing discipline, we will not grow spiritually any more than we would grow physically if we neglected the disciplines of eating, sleeping, and exercising.

If you have any interest whatsoever in fulfilling your spiritual potential, it is essential that you begin to practice advance decision making in your spiritual life. I have discovered three things that I must do if my spiritual life is going to flourish. First, I need to participate regularly in worship services at my church. Second, I need a daily time of personal interaction with the Lord. Third, I need fellowship with other believers in some type of Christian service. If I do not actively participate in these three endeavors, I wilt. I feel spiritually frustrated, and it seems as if God is not using me. Sooner or later every true believer comes to an understanding of what it takes for him or her to flourish as a Christian—the minimum daily or weekly requirements of a healthy spiritual life. And this is where discipline enters in.

When you determine what has to happen on a regular basis for you to flourish in Christ, it is time to make some advance decisions. If in order to grow spiritually you need to be part of the body of Christ when it gathers to worship, make an advance decision to be there—and go. Say, "All right, I *will* be with the body of believers when it assembles. I *will* attend church every Sunday morning." Don't wait until Saturday night when you get in late and then ask, "Do I feel like setting the alarm?" Don't ask, "Who's speaking? What's the message about?" Don't look out the window to see what the weather is like. Go because you have already decided to do so.

In the same way, if you need personal time with the Lord each day, find the time, block it off on your calendar, and keep the appointment. Perhaps you have your devotional time when you get up in the morning, when you arrive at your office, during your lunch hour, or before you go to bed at night. You might spend the time reading the Bible, praying, writing in your journal, or listening to a tape—anything that strengthens you in your walk with the Lord. Structure your time and activities in whatever way best suits your needs, but do not leave your time with the Lord to chance. Make the advance decision to keep your daily appointment with Him, and keep it without fail.

STICKING WITH DISCIPLINE

When you come to the point in your spiritual life of saying, "I'm going to harness the powers of discipline and commit myself to meeting my minimum requirements," you are really saying, "I'll do what it takes. I'm willing to go through the discomfort and pain of the investment stage first so that I can experience the blessedness of flourishing as a Christian the rest of my life." You are making an advance decision to delay gratification as long as necessary to achieve the results you most desire. That's discipline.

The essence of discipline, then, is delayed gratification, and the key to practicing discipline is advance decision making. But some of you are saying, "I can't do this alone." You heartily believe in delayed gratification and you have frequently tried advance decision making, but your efforts fall short. Somehow your high resolves melt in the heat of temptation or the pleasant warmth of laziness.

There's good news: God does not expect you to do it alone. He knows you need brothers and sisters running along with you (in fact, that's one reason Christians come to God as a church and not just as individuals). If you need help in sticking to your decisions, harness the power of accountability. Ask two or three friends to hold you accountable for your decisions. Tell them, "I've made these advance decisions because I really want the payoff. Please hold me to them." This is a tremendous boost to discipline. In addition, God says in His Word that the Holy Spirit helps you produce discipline in your life (Galatians 5:23). You can depend on His aid.

WHAT'S IN THIS FOR ME?

Discipline without rewards would eventually seem rather grim. Fortunately, the payoffs of a disciplined life are enormous. Chicago Bears linebacker Mike Singletary is a member of my church. I have been to his home, and I have seen the impressive collection of training equipment he has set up in his basement. "Mike," I said, "the Bears have tens of thousands of dollars worth of workout equipment at Halas Hall. Why do you want more in your basement?"

"I want to go overboard," Mike told me. "I'm willing to pay any price, because, when game time comes, I want to be ready." That's why, after a full day of practice, Mike often goes home, walks down to his basement, and continues to work out. What are the payoffs for him? Being able to play pro football; playing in the Super Bowl; being named all-pro for three seasons.

The rewards of discipline are great, but they are seldom immediate. When the world clamors for instant gratification and easy solutions, it is hard to choose the way of discipline instead. But you will never build a walk with God, a marriage, a body, or a bank account by obeying the world's law of instant gratification. Payday will come in its own time, if you endure the pain and put your nose to the grindstone now.

STUDY QUESTIONS

1. Can you think of some specific ways that delayed gratification could be applied to your life right now?

2. Advance decision making is vital to making wise decisions when temptation comes calling. Take the following areas of your life and list several decisions for each that should be made in advance: church, work, finances, relationships, physical fitness, time with the Lord.

3. What other areas can you think of that need to have a similar list?

Chapter 19

No More Giving
in to Temptation

By Tony Evans

Great men are they who see that the spiritual
is stronger than any material force.

RALPH WALDO EMERSON

*D*o you remember an old B-grade movie called *The Blob*? As I recall, a meteor came hurtling in from outer space, crashed to earth in a wooded area, and split open. As it lay there glowing, a man came up to it and poked it with a stick. Suddenly and violently, this cosmic goo slithered up the stick and onto the man's arm.

The man began screaming and running, doing all kinds of things to try and get this gluelike substance off his body, but as we watched, the blob began to consume him. The harder he worked to shake off the blob, the more completely he was consumed, until finally, he was gone. This bloblike creature had devoured him.

As the movie went on, the blob got bigger and bigger by consuming everything in its path. Pretty soon, it was eating everyone in town. People were running around screaming because the blob was taking over.

TEMPTATION: A LITTLE GOES A LONG WAY

When I think about temptation, I am reminded of *The Blob*. Like the blob, temptation is pervasive. It didn't matter whether people in the movie wanted to deal with the blob. It was there, and it was coming for them. Their only choice was to run or get blobbed.

That's the way it is with temptation. If you're alive, you're on the list. It's that simple. Temptation will find you.

Now, the blob started off small. It was just an interesting looking lump of glowing goo. The man who poked at it with a stick didn't really feel threatened at that point. He was just curious to see what it was.

Temptation usually starts in a small way too. It's in just one little area. We reach out to touch it and get a little bit of it on us. But when we try to shake it off, we find out it's sticky. No matter what we do, it doesn't let go. In fact, it starts moving up our arms, eating away at us until it consumes us.

Temptation is a fact of life for all of us, Christians as much as unbelievers. The difference is that if you are a child of God, you have supernatural power available to you to say no to temptation and to live a life that pleases our Creator.

Now in case you don't already know, let me give you two pieces of news right up front. The first is that the Bible never condemns you for being a man and having a man's desires. God made you that way. Your desires are normal. You'll take them to the grave with you. So the answer to temptation is not denying who and what you are.

The second piece of news is that the Bible never allows you to make excuses for sin based on your maleness and your normal, God-given desires. Why? Because your *temptations* to sin are not from God (James 1:13–16). And because God has made provision for victory over temptation. Let's talk about it.

Winning the War Against Sin — Step 1: Clean House

Before we became Christians, our flesh was well-trained in evil by the devil and the world, and we developed sinful appetites. Some men may have a propensity for drugs because that's what they were around in their days in the flesh. Others may have a problem with sexual immorality for the same reason.

The flesh is like a magnet that attracts what is evil and against God. What you were exposed to in your life helps to determine what your "magnet" attracts. Some men are worse off than others in this regard because they received Christ at a later age and had a lot of years to indulge their appetites for evil. Even among those who turned to the Lord at a very early age, the flesh still has plenty of chances to express itself. This is true because we all sin every day in the things we say, do, and even think.

Now this is important to understand: When God redeems and justifies us, He does not repair our flesh. He never disconnects the magnet, if you will.

That is the problem with trying to please God in the flesh and making New Year's resolutions and such things. Those are just human attempts to fix the flesh. God has already consigned the flesh to the grave. Someday it will be worm food. Our flesh is so corrupted by sin that it is actually beyond repair. Once you understand this, it will save you from trying to solve your struggle with sin by trying to make your flesh behave.

But in the meantime, becoming a Christian and living like one is like moving into a house where the old inhabitants were dirty and grimy and their filthy things were thrown all over. You move in and start cleaning. You paint the walls, get new carpet and appliances, and eventually the place looks totally different on the inside. It's the same house outside, but it's brand-new on the inside.

That's what God did to our inner person when we became heirs to salvation. You are a brand-new person inside. You may look the same physically, but spiritually the story is different: "If anyone is in Christ, he is a new creation; the old has gone, the new has come!" (2 Corinthians 5:17, NIV).

WINNING THE WAR—
STEP 2: OWNING UP TO YOUR PROBLEM

In this sense, we Christians are true dual personalities. Our redeemed inner self wants to please God, while our sin-contaminated, unredeemed flesh seeks to enslave us again.

Your inner person, which has been made brand-new in the image of God, doesn't want to sin. But your outer person, your old fleshly nature, is used to sinning and doesn't want to stop.

Paul knew there were times when he fell short of pleasing God. There were times when he lost the battle, because he says in Romans 7:23 that sin made him its prisoner. He's being very real and honest about this struggle with sin, and yes, even his defeat at the hands of sin.

This is our problem as much as it was Paul's. We are believers, but our new natures are engaged in a very real struggle with the old flesh for control of our appetites and actions. But notice that Paul does not try to excuse himself or make allowances for sin. He doesn't say, "I just can't help myself. I'm not strong. Everybody else is doing it. I'm a Christian anyway, so one little sin won't hurt."

Instead, he says he knows what the flesh is up to; he

knows it's out to trip him up and enslave him. And he knows he needs to oppose the flesh because he says, "I've got this other law within me that hates what the flesh is trying to do. In my mind and heart, I want to serve God."

WINNING THE WAR —
STEP 3: DEVELOP SPIRITUAL SENSITIVITY

It's the immature Christian who thinks he can handle temptation. It's the carnal Christian who says, "That could never happen to me. I would never fall for that."

The apostle John wrote, "But if we walk in the light, as he is in the light…the blood of Jesus, his Son, purifies us from all sin" (1 John 1:7, NIV). That's a continuous action. Jesus' blood keeps on cleansing us.

How can the blood of Jesus keep on cleansing us from sin as we walk in the light? Because it's only when we walk in the light that we can see our sin. For example, a Christian who is not walking in the light may say that adultery is bad, but that lust is normal. But a Christian who is walking in the light of God's Word says adultery is bad and lust is equally hideous. His sensitivity to sin has grown because he has God's point of view on things. The more of God you see, the more of your own sinfulness you see.

What's the answer to this problem of temptation and sin? How can we get victory over it rather than constantly caving in and excusing our future?

THE HERE-AND-NOW SOLUTION:
THE HOLY SPIRIT

Look at the rest of Romans 7:25: "So then, I myself in my mind am a slave to God's law, but in the sinful nature a slave to the law of sin" (NIV).

Paul says, "I've got two laws working in me. I've got the law of sin telling me, 'Come over here. Do this. Try this. Touch this.' And I've got the law of God saying, 'No, come over here. Do this. Don't do this. Don't touch this.'"

But notice the new law Paul introduces in Romans 8:2: "the law of the Spirit of life." This law or principle, the power of the indwelling Spirit, will keep you from having to obey the law of the flesh. It won't keep you from feeling the desires of the flesh, but it will keep you from having to act on those desires. You may feel like taking illegal drugs, but you don't have to take them. You may feel like practicing immorality, but you don't have to act on that temptation. You may be tempted, but you don't have to yield to the flesh.

Remember our movie *The Blob*? They tried every which way to get rid of that pile of cosmic goo. They shot it and bombed it, but every time they split it into a thousand little pieces, it just grew back together again—that is, until someone haphazardly put some ice on it. They discovered the blob couldn't handle the cold.

So they started spraying the blob with cold things. The cold didn't destroy it, but it did hold it at bay until they could move it to a place where it was perpetually cold. That way, it could never cause trouble again. While they couldn't get rid of the blob, they controlled it by changing its environment.

That's what God wants us to do with our "blob," our propensity to sin. We need to change its environment. We cannot feed the flesh and expect to be victorious in the Spirit. We need to starve the flesh and feed the Spirit, because when we do that, the law of the Spirit will transcend the law of the flesh.

There is no forcing us to sin. The devil is a powerful being, but all he can do is tempt and influence us. If you are feeding the spirit within you through prayer, the study of God's Word, and worship participation in a Bible-teaching church, you can overcome the law of sin and death. If you will starve your flesh by denying it the magazines, books, movies, and other enticements it craves, you can tame your wrong desires.

STUDY QUESTIONS

1. What is the function of the "law of the Spirit of life" Paul is referring to in Romans 8?

2. Because of this "law," Christians have the ability to resist temptation. Do you feel this law at work in your own life? Explain.

3. Cooperation with the Spirit is a key ingredient to victory over temptation. What things can you do that would help you cooperate more fully with the Spirit?

Adapted from *No More Excuses: Be the Man God Made You to Be,* by Tony Evans. Copyright © 1996, pages 133–48. Used by permission of Good News Publishers/Crossway Books, Wheaton, IL 60187.

Chapter 20

An Antidote to Satan's Devices

By Charles Spurgeon

Now the serpent was more subtle than any beast
of the field which the LORD God had made.

GENESIS 3:1, KJV

That old serpent," called the devil, Satan, deceiver, or liar, is the one of whom our Lord Jesus said to the Jews, "When he speaketh a lie, he speaketh of his own: for he is a liar, and the father of it" (John 8:44, KJV). God was pleased in creation to give to many beasts subtlety—to some, cunning combined with strength, and to others, instincts of most marvelous wisdom—for self-preservation and the procuring of food. But all the wise instincts and subtlety of the beasts of the field are far excelled by the subtlety of Satan. Even man, though far more cunning than any mere creature, is no match for the cunning of Satan.

Satan is the master deceiver and is able to overcome us for several reasons. A primary reason that Satan should be cunning is that he is *malicious,* for malice is of all things the most productive of cunning. When a man is revengeful, it is amazing how cunning he is to find opportunities to strike out. When enmity thoroughly possesses his soul and pours its venom into his very blood, he will become exceedingly crafty in the means he uses to provoke and injure his adversary. No, there is no one more full of malice against man than Satan, as he proves every day, and that malice sharpens his inherent wisdom so that he becomes exceedingly subtle.

Satan may well be cunning now—I may truthfully say, more cunning than he was in the days of Adam—for he has had long dealings with the human race. His temptation of Eve was his first occasion of dealing with mankind, but he has long since exercised all his diabolical thought and mighty powers to annoy and ruin men. There is not a saint whom he has not beset and not a sinner whom he has not misled. Together with his troops of evil spirits, he has continually exercised a terrible control over the sons of men; he is therefore well-skilled in all the arts of temptation.

I suppose there is nothing of human nature that Satan cannot unravel. Though, doubtless, he is the biggest fool that has ever existed, yet beyond all doubt, he is the craftiest of fools. I may add, that is no great paradox, for craft is always folly and craftiness is but another shape of departure from wisdom.

First, I shall define the craft and subtlety of Satan and the methods in which Satan attacks our soul. Second, I shall give you a few words of admonition with regard to the wisdom that we must exercise against Satan and the only means that we can use effectually to prevent Satan's subtlety from being the instrument of our destruction.

THE CRAFT AND SUBTLETY OF SATAN

Satan reveals his craft and subtlety by *the methods of his attack.* He does not attack with unbelief and distrustfulness the man who is calm and at ease. Satan attacks such a man in a more vulnerable point than that. Self-love, self-confidence, world-liness—these will be the weapons that Satan will use against him.

I believe that Satan seldom attacks a man in a place of strength, but he generally looks for the weak point, the beset-ting sin. "There," says he, "there will I strike the blow." God help us in the hour of battle and the time of conflict! Indeed, unless the Lord should help us, this crafty foe might easily find enough joints in our armor and soon send the deadly arrow into our soul, so that we should fall down wounded before him.

Take heed to yourselves, therefore: "Put on the whole armour of God" (Ephesians 6:11, KJV); "Be sober, be vigilant; because your adversary the devil, as a roaring lion, walketh about, seeking whom he may devour: whom resist steadfast in the faith" (1 Peter 5:8–9, KJV); and God help you to prevail over him!

A second thing in which Satan discloses his cunning is *the weapons that he will often use against us.* Sometimes he will attack the child of God with past remembrances of the days of his carnal state. At other times, Satan will use the weapon of our own experience. "Ah!" the devil will say, "on such-and-such a day, you sinned in this way. How can you be a child of God?" At another time he will say, "You are self-righteous; therefore, you cannot be an heir of heaven." Then he will begin to rake up all the old stories that we have long forgot-ten of all our past unbeliefs, our past wanderings, and so forth, and throw them in our face. He will say, "What! You,

you a Christian? Some Christian you must be!"

Or possibly he will begin to tempt you by another's example: "So-and-so is a believer; he did it. Why can't you do the same? So-and-so does it, and he gets by and is just as respected as you are." Be careful, for Satan knows how to choose his weapons! He is not coming out against you, if you are a great giant, with a sling and a stone. He comes armed to the teeth to cut you down.

The craftiness of the devil is discovered in another thing: in *the agents the devil employs*. The devil does not do all his dirty work alone; he often employs others to do it for him. When Samson had to be overcome, Satan had a Delilah ready to tempt and lead him astray. Satan knew Samson's heart, where his weakest point was, and he therefore tempted Samson by means of the woman he loved. An old divine says, "There's many a man that has had his head broken by his own rib"; and certainly that is true. Satan has sometimes set a woman's own husband to cast her down to destruction, or he has used some dear friend as the instrument to work his ruin.

Satan shows his cunning by *the times in which he attacks us.* I thought, when I was sick, that if I could only get up from my bed again and be made strong, I would give the devil a most terrible thrashing for the way he attacked me when I was sick. Coward! Why did he not wait till I was well? But I always find that if my spirits sink and I am in a low condition of heart, Satan specially chooses that time to attack me with unbelief. Let him come upon us when the promise of God is fresh in our memory and we are enjoying a time of sweet outpouring of heart in prayer before God, and he will see how we will fight against him then. But no, he knows that then we have the strength to resist him, and prevailing with God, we should be able to prevail over the devil also. He therefore comes upon us when there is a cloud between ourselves and God. When the body is depressed and the spirits are weak, then will he tempt us and try to lead us to distrust God.

WHAT SHALL WE DO WITH THIS ENEMY?

Our desire is to enter the kingdom of heaven, and we cannot enter it while we stand still. The City of Destruction is behind us, and Death pursues us. We must press toward heaven, but in the way there stands this "roaring lion, seeking whom he may devour." What shall we do? He has great subtlety. How shall we overcome him? Shall we seek to be as subtle as he is? That would be a foolish task; indeed, it would be a sinful one. To seek to be crafty, like the devil, would be as wicked as it would be futile. What shall we do then? Shall we attack Satan with wisdom? Alas, our wisdom is but folly! "Vain man would be wise," but at his very best, he is but "like a wild ass's colt" (Job 11:12, KJV). What then shall we do?

The only way to repel Satan's subtlety is by *acquiring true wisdom*. Again I repeat it: Man has none of that in himself. What then? Herein is true wisdom. If you would successfully wrestle with Satan, make the Holy Scriptures your daily commune. Out of this sacred Word continually draw your armor and ammunition. Lay hold upon the glorious doctrines of God's Word; make them your daily meat and drink. So shall you be strong to resist the devil, and you shall be joyful in discovering that he will flee from you.

Above all, if we would successfully resist Satan, we must look not merely to revealed wisdom but to *Incarnate Wisdom*. Here must be the chief place of resort for every tempted soul! We must flee to Him "who of God is made unto us wisdom, and righteousness, and sanctification, and redemption" (1 Corinthians 1:30, KJV). He must teach us, He must guide us, He must be our All-in-all. We must keep close to Him in communion. The sheep are never so safe from the wolf as when they are near the shepherd. We shall never be so secure from the arrows of Satan as when we have our head lying on the Savior's bosom. Believer, walk according to His example, live daily in His fellowship, trust always in His blood, and in this way you shall be more than a conqueror over the subtlety and craft of Satan himself.

It must be a joy to the Christian to know that, in the long run, the craft of Satan shall all be defeated and his evil designs against the saints shall prove of no effect. Are you not looking forward to the day when all your temptations are over and you shall land in heaven? And will you not then look down upon this archenemy with holy laughter and derision? While Satan has sought to destroy the living tree, trying to uproot it, he has only been like a gardener digging with his spade and loosening the earth to help the roots to spread themselves. And when he has been with his ax seeking to lop the Lord's trees and mar their beauty, what has he been, after all, but a pruning knife in the hand of God to take away the branches that do not bear fruit and purge those that do bear some that they might bring forth more fruit?

Once upon a time, you know, the church of Christ was like a little brook flowing along in a little narrow dell. Just a few saints were gathered at Jerusalem, and the devil thought, "Now I'll get a great stone and stop the brook from running." So he went and got the great stone and dashed it down into the middle of the brook, thinking, of course, he would stop it from running. Instead of doing so, he scattered the drops all over the world, and each drop became the mother of a fresh fountain. You know what that stone was: It was persecution, and the saints were scattered by it. But then,

"Therefore they that were scattered abroad went every where preaching the word" (Acts 8:4, KJV), and so the church was multiplied and the devil defeated.

Satan, I tell you to your face, you are the greatest fool that ever breathed, and I will prove it to you in the day when you and I shall stand as enemies—sworn enemies, as we are this day—at the great throne of God. And so may you say to him when he attacks you. Fear him not, but resist him steadfast in the faith, and you shall prevail.

STUDY QUESTIONS

1. What is one area of weakness in your life that Satan finds the easiest to attack?

2. What is one strength in your life that you feel is the most difficult for Satan to penetrate?

3. What are two of the greatest weapons the Christian has at his disposal to fight Satan?

Taken from *Spiritual Warfare in a Believer's Life*, by Charles Spurgeon. Copyright © 1993 by Lance Wubbels, ed. Published by Emerald Books. Used by permission.

SECTION THREE

Sexual Purity

If you have received the Spirit and are obeying him,
you find he brings your spirit into complete harmony
with God, and the sound of your goings and the
sound of God's going are one and the same.

OSWALD CHAMBERS

If you make a compromise with surrender,
you can remain interested in the abundant life,
all the riches of freedom, love, and peace,
but it is the same as looking at a display in a shop window. You look
through the window but do not go in and buy. You will not pay the
price—surrender [to Christ].

E. STANLEY JONES

Good thoughts bear good fruit, bad thoughts bear
bad fruit—and man is his own gardener.

JAMES ALLEN

Obedience means marching right on
whether we feel like it or not.
Many times we go against our feelings.
Faith is one thing, feeling is another.

DWIGHT L. MOODY

Sexual Impurity: Countering the Devastating Epidemic

BY BRUCE WILKINSON

No matter how many pleasures Satan offers you,
his ultimate intention is to ruin you.
Your destruction is his highest priority.

ERWIN W. LUTZER

*D*o you remember the first day you saw one? It may have been your older brother's, or you may have stumbled across it underneath some old boxes in your dad's closet or drawer. Or maybe you found it amid a pile of junk you were playing around in an abandoned field. You couldn't believe it. She had no clothes on! I mean, none. And was she ever beautiful. The most perfect woman you could ever imagine.

That first time wasn't a formal choice. It was perhaps an innocent exposure to pornography. But then you hid it. Probably right near where you found it, but a bit more out of sight. And planned when you could sort of find yourself back in this same neck of the woods again....

But now life is different, isn't it? Instead of having to hide in the woods, it's right in your face. At every turn. And more powerful and compelling. More erotic because that all-too-beautiful woman now has come off the page and right onto the rented videotape. Or the cable network, or miraculously from the "heavens" with your satellite dish. Or off the Internet. One national news magazine recently reported that in one month one pornographic site received more than 6 million hits—6 million!

This one is the big one, isn't it? The most recent statistics capture the scope of this epidemic—more than six out of ten Christian men openly admit they have a problem with sexual immorality. For men, there isn't any other major sin that even comes close to this epidemic.

HOW BAD IS IT?

How are we doing in this fight? Go back ten years—how would it compare to today? How about twenty years? Fifty years?

This epidemic is spreading like wildfire, and the fire has discovered that it burns just as well in churches as in local bars. You see, what burns isn't the lumber of buildings, but the lusts of men. Wherever men are to be found, the epidemic is raging rampant with no signs of burning out or burning up. Burn victims are everywhere.

Times are different, but the lusts of men aren't. The apostle Paul wrote to men and women whose society was even more immoral than this one and captured the essence about God's will and your sexuality: "For this is the will of God, your sanctification: that you should abstain from sexual immorality" (1 Thessalonians 4:3).

Have you ever wondered, "I wish I knew what the will of God is for my life"? This is the most direct answer in all the

Bible to that question. The will of God is your sanctification (which has the same root word as *holiness*)—specifically, that you would abstain from sexual immorality. Sanctification refers to the process of being holy and set apart unto God for His service.

As you read through the Bible, you cannot miss the major importance our sexuality has, not only for us and others, but also for God Himself. If men and women do not get their sexuality under God's control, they will not be able to become people of holiness. Sexual immorality is a threshold sin. On one side of the threshold is immorality and on the other is purity. On one side are guilt, lying, deceit, addiction, and shame, and on the other side are freedom, honesty, transparency, liberty, and a clear conscience. Believers who are in bondage to immorality find that unless they experience victory in this area, they cannot grow in holiness or serve the Lord with passion and power.

How to Get Under God's Control

At times people comment that the Bible is an old-fashioned, out-of-date, prudish book that never deals with the real nitty-gritty problems of twenty-first-century life. When I hear that, I always find myself wondering if they've ever truly looked through the Bible, because it seems that it is usually more straightforward and right-on about modern-day problems than any contemporary newspaper, magazine, or newsletter. Here's what it has to say:

> But because of immoralities, let each man have his own wife, and let each woman have her own husband. Let the husband fulfill his duty to his wife, and likewise also the wife to her husband. The wife does

not have authority over her own body, but the husband does; and likewise also the husband does not have authority over his own body, but the wife does. Stop depriving one another, except by agreement for a time that you may devote yourselves to prayer, and come together again lest Satan tempt you because of your lack of self-control. (1 Corinthians 7:2–5, NASB)

The two major problems with men in their sexual lives have to do with "sexual immorality" and "self-control." Did you notice that these verses use the words "because of immoralities" and "because of your lack of self-control"? God's answer for both issues is the very subject of this paragraph! In fact, I believe that the Bible teaches that both issues—sexual immorality and self-control—are to be solved with the same God-given solution.

What is that solution? "Let each man have his own wife, and let each woman have her own husband." The marriage relationship is God's primary provision for your sexual drives and their full expression and satisfaction. It's very interesting that both times the word *have* is used in this verse, it is in the imperative. This isn't an option or a suggestion, but a command. Because of sexual immorality, God wants you to have your own wife. (Unless, of course, you have been given the gift of "singleness," which I would surmise to be an unusual gift.)

Now, why would God say the solution to sexual immoralities (various kinds and multiple temptations) is your wife or husband? Because the proper fulfillment of your sex drive and your emotional love and affection is to be solidly focused in the person of your wife. When God created humans, He created both male and female, and from the beginning, God created one woman for one man. Not multiple women for one man and not men for men, but one woman for one man for life.

But What About the Inside?

Unfortunately, marriage controls only the external sins of immorality. There are also internal sins of immorality that can't be controlled by external means.

In Colossians 2:20–22, Paul scolds the Colossian church for subjecting themselves "to regulations...according to the commandments and doctrines of men." These people were trying to be very pious and do the right things to earn the favor of men. But Paul saw right through it and said, "These things indeed have an appearance of wisdom in self-imposed religion, false humility, and neglect of the body, but are of no value against the indulgence of the flesh" (v. 23).

The flesh is an enemy of God that lives inside you. It's an internal power that is with you wherever you go, but it can't be defeated by external forces.

However, Paul not only admonishes the Colossian church, he also tells them how to defeat this vicious adversary:

> If then you were raised with Christ, seek those things which are above, where Christ is, sitting at the right hand of God. Set your mind on things above, not on things on the earth. (Colossians 3:1–2)

If you've accepted Christ as your personal Savior, you have been raised with Christ into a new life, and you've taken the first step in defeating the flesh. Next, Paul commands you to "seek those things which are above." To clarify, Paul says it another way in Galatians 5:16: "I say then: Walk in the Spirit, and you shall not fulfill the lust of the flesh."

Victory over your flesh, and thus victory over sexual temptation, is accomplished by living in the Spirit. Don't focus so much on your flesh—focus on the Spirit and the Word of God, which He will illuminate. In fact, Romans 8:5 shares this truth: "For those who live according to the flesh *set their minds on* the things of the flesh, but those who live according to the Spirit, *[set their minds on]* the things of the Spirit."

So one question you may ask yourself as you seek victory over sexual temptation is, How much do you think about the Holy Spirit? Do you "grieve" Him by your sinful thoughts and "quench" Him by your willful neglect of His wishes? Only by becoming a man of the Spirit can you become a man "not of the flesh."

Chapter 21

Fighting the Good Fight

By Steve Farrar

Create in me a clean heart, O God,
and renew a steadfast spirit within me.

PSALM 51:10

While speaking at a men's conference I met a group of guys who were all in the same accountability group. They asked if we might get together for a few minutes. I knew from our initial conversation that they came from two different churches, and I had a pretty strong clue about what they wanted to discuss.

Both churches had senior pastors who had been asked to step down because of moral failure in their personal lives. Those failures had devastated both churches, sending Richter-scale shock waves up and down their part of the country.

Both pastors had very high profiles. Both were remarkably gifted speakers who could mesmerize people with their humor, exposition, and personalities. Thousands of people were coming to hear each one, which is why their fall was so cataclysmic. They affected many people as they climbed the ladder, and they affected even more when they fell off.

I had met both of these men fifteen years earlier. After spending an afternoon with the first pastor, I remember being somewhat stunned as I drove home. As Mary and I talked over dinner, I told her a little bit of our conversation. Although we had just met, a mutual friend with whom he felt very comfortable was with us, so his guard was down. At dinner that night I said something that really surprised my wife.

"Mary, I think that guy is headed for a major fall."

I'm no prophet, but something was obviously wrong. The signals were so clear that even I could see them. This guy talked freely of his dreams, his aspirations, the books he was reading, his latest successes. Clearly, he had a number of influences in his life, but the New Testament apparently wasn't one of them. He sounded like a guy looking to get to the top, in a hurry.

That's what he did, but he got there so fast that he fell off. It happened ten years after our meeting. After allegations of sexual involvement with a female associate he divorced his wife and left his children.

I had met the other pastor about a year later, and we spent an entire weekend together. What a great weekend that was! This guy had a love for Jesus Christ and a love for the Scriptures that was very apparent. He also talked about his wife throughout the weekend, and how they were so very careful to protect and sustain their marriage.

This guy was solid, the exact opposite of the other pastor. I greatly benefited from our time together and wished that it could have continued. That's why I was absolutely shocked to hear that he had resigned from his church for moral reasons.

In fact, I didn't believe it until I talked with his associate and the facts were confirmed.

FIGHTIN' FOR THE BRAND

The Christian life is a violent life. It is a life of warfare, of high-stakes spiritual combat. The Bible clearly states that we are in a battle with the world, the flesh, and the devil. That's precisely why Paul told Timothy to "fight the good fight."

Satan may be many things, but he is no fool. His efforts are very strategic. If a highly visible spiritual leader can be brought down, the fallout will be great. That's why we should be praying for our pastors and for other leaders in ministry. It's also why we should be praying for ourselves.

You don't have to be a well-known speaker to be attacked. The enemy is more than happy to bring down a Sunday school teacher or any other person of influence in a local congregation.

The question that these brokenhearted church leaders put before me that evening was this: "How is it that men who have such influence in the body of Christ can suddenly fall into sexual immorality?"

The answer I offered was that it probably wasn't sudden. It seemed sudden, but only because we couldn't see the private choices these men had been making over the previous years. Sexual immorality is usually the tragic result of a series of poor and very private choices.

That's why Paul's words to Timothy have such relevance. In fact, it is impossible to climb the character ladder without applying these words to our lives.

This command I entrust to you, Timothy, my son, in accordance with the prophecies previously made concerning you, that by them you may fight the good fight. (1 Timothy 1:18, NASB)

THE MENTORING EPISTLES

First and Second Timothy, along with Titus, are frequently called the Pastoral Epistles. Timothy and Titus were young pastors, and Paul wrote to them to give some tangible principles. Today, we might say that Paul was mentoring these young men.

What is a mentor? John Gardner says a mentor is an older person who actively helps young people along the road to leadership—a friend, an advisor, a teacher, a coach, a listener. "Mentoring may be as formal as a master-apprentice relationship or as informal as an older friend helping a younger one."

If you ever benefited from the wisdom and counsel of an older person, you know firsthand how meaningful a mentor can be. People who have profited from that kind of relationship also make excellent mentors themselves.

Paul and Timothy had a father-son relationship. They were exceptionally close and Paul had a vested interest in Timothy's well-being. Timothy was not happy. He was in over his head at Ephesus. But Paul needed Timothy to do at least three things: appoint elders, combat false doctrine and false teachers, and supervise the church as Paul's personal representative. That was a tall order for a young man.

Really, Timothy's main problem was that he wasn't Paul. He didn't have Paul's age or wisdom or in-your-face personality. Timothy was a nonconfronter in a situation that cried out for confrontation.

NO PLACE TO RUN

That's why, earlier in the chapter, in verse 3, Paul had to urge Timothy to "remain on at Ephesus" (NASB). Timothy didn't want to stick around, but Paul wanted him to "fight the good fight." It was time for Timothy to stand tall.

Mentors know when their protégés need some encouragement. That's why Paul reminded Timothy of the prophecies that were made concerning him. We are not privy to those, but apparently someone had predicted the kind of ministry Timothy would have. These prophecies were a source of encouragement to the young pastor. That's why Paul brought them up.

Paul was Timothy's coach. It's almost as though Paul, writing from a distance, was trying to psych Timothy up for the game, not unlike a coach in a locker room. Paul wanted Timothy to get in there and fight!

I remember very well the first root canal I ever had. I was twelve years old, and my tooth started to abscess one night as we were eating dinner. My mom called the dentist and took me right in. As I was stepping into that room, Cassius Clay was stepping into the ring to meet Sonny Liston. It was Tuesday evening, February 25, 1964. My dentist had the fight going full blast on the radio as he worked on me.

This was the first big fight of Clay's career. We now know him as Muhammad Ali, one of the greatest fighters of all time. But on that night, he was just a young, loudmouthed kid against the man known as the "The Bear." Before the fight I saw a full-page picture of Sonny Liston and thought to myself, *That guy is the meanest and toughest I've ever seen. Cassius Clay will get killed!*

That was pretty much the consensus before the fight. I didn't think I'd survive the root canal or that Clay would survive Liston, but I was wrong on both counts. My dentist knocked out the nerve and Clay knocked out the bear.

Timothy was no Cassius Clay, yet he was called to "fight

the good fight." And so are we. We are called to fight it every day. But here's the question—and it is extremely important.

How do you fight the good fight, especially when so many in the body of Christ are not doing so? They have been disqualified and have not gone the distance. So how do you do it?

Paul gives the answer: "keeping faith and a good conscience, which some have rejected and suffered shipwreck in regard to their faith" (1 Timothy 1:19, NASB).

KEEPING FAITH AND A GOOD CONSCIENCE

In other words, you have to do both. If you just keep faith, you won't fight the good fight. If you just keep a good conscience, you won't fight the good fight. So let's take them in order.

"Keeping faith"

What in the world does that mean? Well, where does faith come from? Ephesians 2:8 is very clear that faith is a gift of God. But how does God distribute this faith? Through what means does faith come into our lives? According to Romans 10:17: "Faith comes from hearing, and hearing by the word of Christ" (NASB).

And what is the Word of God? Hebrews 4:12 says, the "word of God is living and active and sharper than any two-edged sword, and piercing as far as the division of soul and spirit, of both joints and marrow, and able to judge the thoughts and intentions of the heart" (NASB).

When Paul instructs Timothy to fight the good fight by "keeping faith," Paul is referring to the doctrinal purity that comes only from the Word of God. He is reminding Timothy that he must stay in the Word if his faith is going to remain clear, clean, and pure.

Mark this: If you're not in the Word it is *impossible* for you to fight the good fight. Moses certainly didn't downplay Scripture. Note his words in Deuteronomy 32:46–47: "Take to your heart all the words which I am warning you today, which you shall command your sons to observe carefully, even all the words of this law. For it is not an idle word for you; indeed *it is your life*" (NASB).

That's a pretty strong statement, but it fits perfectly with what Jesus said about the character of Scripture. When Jesus was tempted by Satan in the wilderness, He responded to the first temptation with the words, "It is written, Man shall not live by bread alone, but on every word that proceeds out of the mouth of God" (Matthew 4:4, NASB).

We must live off Scripture. It must be our life. The Word of God contains the spiritual vitamins and minerals we need. Without the nutrition of Scripture it is impossible to fight well—no vitality, no energy, no health. No wonder Oswald Chambers said:

> The mere reading of the Word of God has power to communicate the life of God to us mentally, morally, and spiritually. God makes the words of the Bible a sacrament, i.e., the means whereby we partake of His life…

"A good conscience"

Paul also emphasized that we must keep *"a good conscience."* This war is fought on two fronts simultaneously. If you put all of your effort into keeping faith, you will leave your flank wide open. But if you focus completely on keeping a good conscience you are just as vulnerable. To fight the good fight we have to do both. We have to keep faith *and* a good conscience. At the same time.

The priority of a good conscience is a theme Paul rides hard all the way through this letter to Timothy. That makes complete sense, since 1 Timothy is really a handbook on spiritual leadership. It's impossible to be an effective spiritual leader without paying attention to your conscience.

Those who say "Let conscience be your guide" do not have it quite right. The guide to right and wrong is Scripture. Conscience is a nerve that begins to pulsate when we depart from what we know is right. As we move from right toward wrong, conscience sends messages. It lets us know something is wrong. It warns us that we are moving into dangerous territory.

There is a tragic explanation in 1 Timothy of something that is going to happen in the last days. In 1 Timothy 4:1, Paul says: "The Spirit explicitly says that in later times some will fall away from the faith, paying attention to deceitful spirits and doctrines of demons" (NASB).

What is interesting here is the reason some will fall away. Instead of listening to the doctrinal purity of the Word of God, they have paid attention to deceitful spirits and doctrines of demons! But in the next verse Paul explains how. They listened to false teachers, "by means of the hypocrisy of liars *seared in their own conscience* as with a branding iron" (v. 2, NASB).

Did you catch what Paul said? These men can teach such doctrinal deceit, which they *know* to be wrong, because they are men without conscience. It's almost as though they took a white-hot poker and thrust it deep into the depths of their souls. They cauterized their own consciences and they don't feel anything anymore.

Every time the Spirit of God impresses our conscience and we fail to respond to His prompting, we are coating that sensitive nerve with another layer of resistance. Over time, our consciences become hard and callus.

That is a very dangerous state. It is possible for that nerve to become so callus that, when the Holy Spirit touches it, it feels absolutely nothing. Not one impulse.

That, my friends, is a graphic description of a man or woman whose right and wrong "sensitivity transmitters" simply do not work anymore. And they are everywhere.

The key to keeping a good conscience is not so much in the big choices, but the little ones. That's why we are so shocked when we hear about the immorality of a public preacher. Perhaps we have benefited from that person's teachings over the radio or through cassettes. But you can't look into someone's conscience over the radio. You can't look into a conscience at all, where the real fight takes place. Only the Holy Spirit, the enemy, and the person himself are able to see into that very private arena.

Standing tall in private is just as important as standing tall in public. Maybe more so.

Deceit and sexual immorality always go hand in hand. Because before we deceive others we deceive ourselves. Before we lie to others we lie to ourselves. And that's where heeding the first impulses of the Holy Spirit can save us from choices that will completely unravel our lives. Lying must be nipped in the bud.

THREE SHIPS THAT NEVER SAILED HOME

What do the *Titanic,* the *Hymenaeus,* and the *Alexander* have in common? All three experienced horrible shipwrecks. But only the *Titanic* was a ship. Hymenaeus and Alexander were men.

The *Titanic* has been found at the bottom of the Atlantic. Hymenaeus and Alexander can be found in the pages of the

New Testament. Specifically in 1 Timothy:

> Keeping faith and a good conscience, which some
> have rejected and suffered shipwreck in regard to their
> faith. Among these are Hymenaeus and Alexander,
> whom I have delivered over to Satan, so that they may
> be taught not to blaspheme. (1:19–20, NASB)

Shipwrecks are always great tragedies, but to shipwreck spiritually is the greatest tragedy of all. That's what happened to Hymenaeus and Alexander. And it's happening with increasing frequency in the church today.

We are missing a great deal of the story of Hymenaeus and Alexander. But Paul knew the missing pieces, and so did Timothy. They shipwrecked for one of two reasons:

- They didn't keep sound doctrine.
- They didn't keep a good conscience.

Yet there is more than one way to be shipwrecked. And in the body of Christ, the number of shipwrecks attributed to sexual immorality grows every day. Paul wanted Timothy to fight the good fight. That's why he put such emphasis on keeping faith and a good conscience. Both must be well in hand; our walk must back up our talk.

The same questions burned in the minds of the six men I met with at the men's conference: "How in the world did our pastor get involved in immorality?" I reminded them of the morning session, in which I had taught the concepts and the passages in this chapter. As we thought through each set of circumstances, the answers started to emerge.

The first pastor shipwrecked because he had not kept faith. He became enamored with popular psychology. His love for the Scripture gradually gave way to the desire to speak "relevant" messages in the pulpit. He shipwrecked because he lost his love for the purity of the Word, and as he lost his commitment to Scripture, his conscience started to give way as well.

The second pastor was on the other end of the spectrum. He loved the Scriptures, but he got into compromising situations. When a close friend approached him, he explained all this away as harmless. I'm sure that the Holy Spirit also approached him over the years, but he didn't respond. He was doctrinally pure but he still shipwrecked.

Both of these men were gifted. That's why some are attempting to get them back into ministry, even with minimal repentance. "They are so gifted!" comes the reply. No doubt, but the issue is not giftedness. It is character.

John Luther states the matter brilliantly:

Good character is more to be praised than...talent. Most talents are...a gift. Good character, by contrast, is not given to us. We have to build it piece by piece, thought by thought, choice by choice, which requires great courage and determination.

Let me be very direct. If you are involved in some type of sexual sin, please don't take a stand against homosexuality in your community. Please don't attend a school board meeting and speak against a sex education curriculum. And please...don't join a church board or teach a Sunday school class. Because your sin will find you out. And when it does, the moral stands you took will be discredited.

And so will the name of Jesus Christ.

If there is any kind of sin in your life that you have not

confessed, then it is impossible for you to fight the good fight. You may fight, but it won't be the good fight.

And that's no fight at all.

STUDY QUESTIONS

1. Review Peter's strong counsel in 1 Peter 5:1–11. What are three or four key principles that the apostle offers for fighting the good fight?

2. When have you benefited most from a concerned older person willing to stay in your corner? When have you longed for such an individual, but not found one?

3. Reflect on a time when you attempted to "stuff" the voice of your conscience. Were you successful? What was the result?

Taken from *Standing Tall* by Steve Farrar. Copyright © 1994, 2001 by Steve Farrar. Multnomah Publishers, Sisters, OR. Used by permission.

Chapter 22

Discipline of Purity

By R. Kent Hughes

The passions are like fire, useful in a thousand ways
and dangerous only in one, through their excess.

CHRISTIAN NESTELL BOVEE

One need turn on the television for only a few minutes to feel the heat of the oppressive sensuality of our day. Most of the oppression is crude. A boring trip around the TV channels at midday invariably reveals at least one couple wrapped in bed sheets and much sensual monotony.

But the heat has become increasingly artful, especially if its purpose is to sell. The camera focuses close up, in black and white, on an intense, lusting male face, over which is superimposed an amber flame, which then becomes a glowing bottle of Calvin Klein's Obsession, as the face intones its desire. The sticky steam of sensuality penetrates everything in our world!

And the church has not escaped. Recently, *Leadership* magazine commissioned a poll of a thousand pastors. The pastors indicated that 12 percent of them had committed adultery while in the ministry—one out of eight pastors!—and 23 percent had done something they considered sexually inappropriate.

Christianity Today surveyed a thousand of its subscribers who were not pastors and found the figure to be nearly double, with 23 percent saying they had had extramarital intercourse and 45 percent indicating they had done something they themselves deemed sexually inappropriate.

One in four Christian men are unfaithful, and nearly one half have behaved unbecomingly! Shocking statistics! Especially when we remember that *Christianity Today* readers tend to be college-educated church leaders, elders, deacons, Sunday school superintendents, and teachers. If this is so for the Church's leadership, how much higher would these statistics be among the average members of the congregation? Only God knows!

This leads us to an inescapable conclusion: The contemporary evangelical church, broadly considered, is "Corinthian" to the core. It is being stewed in the molten juices of its own sensuality so that it is:

- no wonder the church has lost its grip on holiness.
- no wonder it is so slow to discipline its members.
- no wonder it is dismissed by the world as irrelevant.
- no wonder so many of its children reject it.
- no wonder it has lost its power in many places, and that Islam and other false religions are making so many converts.

Sensuality is easily the biggest obstacle to godliness among men today and is wreaking havoc in the church.

Godliness and sensuality are mutually exclusive, and those in the grasp of sensuality can never rise to godliness while in its sweaty grip. If we are to "discipline [ourselves] for the purpose of godliness" (1 Timothy 4:7, NASB), we must begin with the discipline of purity. There has to be some holy heat, some holy sweat!

Lessons from a Fallen King

Where are we to turn for help? The most instructive example in all of God's Word is the experience of King David, as it is told in 2 Samuel 11.

Life at the Top

As the account begins, David is at the summit of his brilliant career—as high as any man in biblical history. From childhood he had been a passionate lover of God and has possessed an immense integrity of soul, as attested by Samuel's words when he anointed him as king: "Man looks at the outward appearance, but the LORD looks at the heart" (1 Samuel 16:7, NASB). God liked what He saw. God liked David's heart!

His was a brave heart, as was evidenced when he met Goliath and returned the giant's fearsome rhetoric with some spine-tingling words of his own, then charged full-speed into battle, nailing Goliath right between the headlights (1 Samuel 17:45–49).

David had an archetypal sanguine personality brimming with joy, enthusiasm, and confidence, and overflowing with irresistible charisma. David hardly seemed a candidate for moral disaster. But the king was vulnerable, for there were definite flaws in his conduct which left him open to tragedy.

Desensitization

Second Samuel 5, which records David's initial assumption of power in Jerusalem, mentions almost as an aside that "after he left Hebron, David took more concubines and wives in Jerusalem" (v. 13, NIV). We must note, and note well, that David's taking additional wives was sin! Deuteronomy 17, which set down the standards for Hebrew kings, commanded that they refrain from three things: 1) acquiring many horses, 2) taking many wives, and 3) accumulating much silver and gold (see vv. 14–17). David did fine on one and three, but he completely failed on number two by willfully collecting a considerable harem.

We must understand that a progressive desensitization to sin and a consequent inner descent from holiness had taken root in David's life. David's collection of wives, though it was "legal" and not considered adultery in the culture of the day, was nevertheless sin. King David's sensual indulgence desensitized him to God's holy call in his life, as well as to the danger and consequences of falling. In short, David's embrace of socially permitted sensuality desensitized him to God's call and made him easy prey for the fatal sin of his life.

Men, it is the "legal" sensualities, the culturally acceptable indulgences, which will take us down. The long hours of indiscriminate TV watching, which is not only culturally cachet but is expected of the American male, is a massive culprit of desensitization. The expected male talk—double entendre, coarse humor, laughter at things which ought to make us blush—is another deadly agent. Acceptable sensualities have insidiously softened Christian men, as statistics will attest. A man who succumbs to desensitization of the "legal" sensualities is primed for a fall.

Relaxation

The second flaw in David's conduct which opened him to disaster was his relaxation from the rigors and discipline which had been part of his active life. David was at midlife, about fifty years old, and his military campaigns had been so successful, it was not necessary for him to personally go off to war. He rightly gave the "mopping-up" job to his capable general, Joab—and then relaxed. The problem was, his relaxation extended to his moral life. It is hard to maintain inner discipline when you are relaxing in this way. David was imminently vulnerable.

David did not suspect anything unusual was going to happen on that fatal spring day. He did not get up and say, "My, what a beautiful day. I think I will commit adultery today!" May this lesson not be wasted on us, men. Just when we think we are the safest, when we feel no need to keep our guard up, to work on our inner integrity, to discipline ourselves for godliness—temptation will come!

Fixation

It had been a warm day, and evening was falling. The king strode out on the rooftop for some cool air and a look at his city at dusk. As he gazed, his eye caught the form of an unusually beautiful woman who was bathing without modesty. As to how beautiful she was, the Hebrew is explicit: The woman was "very beautiful in appearance" (2 Samuel 11:2, NASB). She was young, in the flower of life, and the evening shadows made her even more enticing. The king looked at her…and he continued to look. After the first glance, David should have turned the other way and retired to his chamber, but he did not. His *look* became a soulful stare and then a burning, libidinous, sweaty *leer.* In that moment David, who had been a man after God's own heart, became a dirty, leering old man. A lustful fixation came over him that would not be denied.

Men, the truth demands some serious questions: Do you have an illicit fixation which has become all you can see? Is the most real thing in your life your desire? If so, you are in deep trouble. Some decisive steps are necessary, as we shall see.

Rationalization

From deadly fixation, King David descended to the next level down, which is rationalization. When his intent became apparent to his servants, one tried to dissuade him, saying, "Isn't this Bathsheba, the daughter of Eliam and the wife of Uriah the Hittite?" (2 Samual 11:3, NIV). But David would not be rebuffed. Some massive rationalization took place in David's mind, perhaps very much as J. Allan Peterson has suggested in *The Myth of the Greener Grass:*

> Uriah is a great soldier, but he's probably not much of a husband or a lover—years older than she is—and he'll be away for a long time. This girl needs a little comfort in her loneliness. This is one way I can help her. No one will get hurt. I do not mean anything wrong by it. This is not lust—I have known that many times. This is love. This is not the same as finding a prostitute on the street. God knows that. And to the servant, "Bring her to me."

The mind controlled by lust has an infinite capacity for rationalization.

- "How can something that has brought such enjoyment be wrong?"
- "God's will for me is to be happy; certainly He would not deny me anything which is essential to my happiness—and this is it!"
- "The question here is one of love. I'm acting in love—the highest love."
- "My marriage was never God's will in the first place."
- "You Christians and your narrow, judgmental attitudes make me sick. You are judging me. You are a greater sinner than I'll ever be!"

Degeneration (Adultery, Lies, Murder)

David's progressive *desensitization, relaxation, fixation,* and *rationalization* set him up for one of the greatest falls in history, and his degeneration. "Then David sent messengers to get her. She came to him, and he slept with her. (She had purified herself from her uncleanness.) Then she went back home. The woman conceived and sent word to David, saying, 'I am pregnant'" (2 Samuel 11:4–5, NIV). David was unaware he had stepped off the precipice and was falling, and that reality would soon arrive. The bottom was coming up fast.

We are all familiar with David's despicable behavior, as he became a calculating liar and murderer in arranging Uriah's death to cover his sin with Bathsheba. Suffice it to say that at this time in the king's life, Uriah was a better man drunk than David was sober (v. 13)!

A year later, David would repent under the withering accusation of the prophet Nathan. But the miserable consequences could not be undone.

The Will of God: Purity

Sometimes people under the Christian umbrella simply do not buy what I am saying in regard to purity. They consider such teaching to be Victorian and puritanical. Victorian it is not. Puritanical it gloriously is, for it is supremely biblical. In answering such people, I take them to the most explicit call for sexual purity I know: 1 Thessalonians 4:3–8.

If the reading of this passage is not convincing enough concerning the biblical ethic, we must understand that it is based on Leviticus 19:2 (NIV), where God says, "Be holy because I, the LORD your God, am holy"—a command which is given in the context of warnings against sexual deviation. I also want to point out that in 1 Thessalonians we are called to avoid sexual immorality and are three times called to be "holy." To reject this is to sin against the Holy Spirit—the living presence of God—as the Thessalonians passage makes so clear.

Men, if we are Christians, it is imperative that we live pure, godly lives in the midst of our Corinthian, "pornotopian" culture. We must live above the horrifying statistics, or the church will become increasingly irrelevant and powerless, and our children will leave it. The church can have no power apart from purity.

STUDY QUESTIONS

1. How many hours of TV do you watch each week? Do you think this has desensitized you to sin? Explain.

2. How much time do you spend each week in leisure? Is it productive leisure that refreshes you, or is it leisure that takes you away from the disciplined life?

3. Before moving to the next chapter, write down several things that you think might produce "holy sweat."

Adapted from *Disciplines of a Godly Man*, by R. Kent Hughes. Copyright © 1991, pages 23–33. Used by permission of Good News Publishers/Crossway Books, Wheaton, IL 60187.

Chapter 23

Leading a Secret
Thought Life

By Patrick Morley

The secret thoughts of a man run over all things, holy, profane,
clean, obscene, grave and light, without shame or blame.

THOMAS HOBBES

We take captive every thought to make it obedient to Christ.

2 CORINTHIANS 10:5, NIV

Are you living a secret thought life significantly different from the "you" that is known by others? Would you be embarrassed if your friends and associates knew what went on inside your mind? If your thoughts were audible, would your wife want a divorce?

Each of us leads a secret thought life, an invisible life known only to us. It is not known to others. This secret life is usually very different from the visible you—the you that is known by others. Yet it is the *real you*—the you that is known by our God.

For some of us, our secret thought life consists of a dreamworld of fantasies which concocts intricate plans that would make us wealthy, famous, and powerful. Others of us fabricate chance meetings with beautiful women who seduce us. We each invent a secret image of how we wish we were, which we would be embarrassed for others to know.

Some of us boil in a hate-world filled with bitterness and resentment over a life that hasn't turned out like we planned. We seethe with jealousy and envy over the lucky break the other fellow had dumped in his lap. We find the words of the rich man contemptible to us, not because the words are wrong, but because we despise him for his success.

There doesn't seem to be any relief from the perpetual stream of negative thoughts which flows through our minds. Because our secret thought life is so sensitive, far too little attention has been devoted to the subject. Why do men lead a secret thought life? What is happening up there in the recesses of our minds?

THE BATTLE FOR THE MIND

One morning I was driving to speak at a men's Bible study. I like driving alone; it's one of the few places where I can think without those incessant interruptions that break my train of thought.

The thick traffic flowed steadily. As I slowed for a traffic light, I was relieved to see that I would make it through the intersection on the next green light. As I braked, the car next to me saw a "hairline crack" in front of me and, without warning, swerved over. I slammed on the brakes and checked the rear-view mirror. So far so good. Anger swept over me but, since I was on my way to speak at a Bible study, I quickly recovered and kept my spiritual glow. I even forgave the bum for being such a spiritual degenerate.

The light turned green and the long line inched toward the intersection. Guess who was the last car to make it through the light? You guessed it! He made it, but I was stuck first in line at the red light. That did it for me, Bible study or not! I let out an audible expletive that came from a part of me not surrendered to God.

If this were an isolated incident, then I would not be too concerned. But every day we each battle for control of our minds. A continual war between good and evil, right and wrong, rages for control of our thought life. The real battlefield for the Christian is the mind.

CONCEALING SIN

Tom's hobby was girl-watching. Whenever he traveled, the part he enjoyed most was sitting in the airport terminal and checking out the women who came and went. After Tom became a Christian, he sensed his obsession displeased God, but it was his one private secret. "Besides," he reasoned, "everyone's entitled to a minor vice, aren't they? Nobody gets hurt. It's a victimless crime."

When we do cross over the line and sin, what should we do about it? "He who conceals his sins does not prosper, but whoever confesses and renounces them finds mercy" (Proverbs 28:13, NIV).

No secrets are kept from God; He knows every word we will speak before it is even on our lips. No one else may know, but God knows. The goal of our secret thought life, since it is no secret from God, should be to live a life of personal holiness. Why do we seem to have such a struggle to conquer our thoughts?

VISIBILITY TO OTHERS

I would rather go to jail than be seen in a bar. Frankly, the reasons are not spiritual, but selfish. I don't want my reputation to be tarnished, so I categorically avoid bars. This has less to do with what Jesus might think than what my friends might think.

The *visibility* of our speech and actions helps us keep these in line. Visibility brings a certain level of self-discipline. Sometimes I think peer pressure actually influences us more to live righteously than the fear of a holy God. We all want to get along with others and have a good reputation, and these ambitions keep our behavior in check.

The nonbeliever doesn't have control of his *high-visibility* sins because he doesn't have the Holy Spirit to make him aware of his sins and bring him under conviction, nor does he have the peer pressure of a church family.

Of course, the peer pressure of visibility isn't bad. If no peer pressure existed, then I would have no accountability; and the temptation to sin would be more alluring (although I'm not suggesting that going in a bar in and of itself is a sin).

But the *low visibility* of our thought life has no peer pressure, no accountability of any sort, save our own self-discipline and dependence upon the Spirit, by which we are forced to pass muster. The result of low visibility? We lead a secret, often unruly, thought life, which we would find embarrassing for others to know about.

AWARENESS BY ME

While others may take note of our sins because of their visibility, we may be aware or unaware of our own sins.

As new Christians, we brought all of our excess baggage with us to our newfound faith. Regrettably, we were full of anger, resentment, bitterness, self-centeredness, lust, envy, and jealousy.

Even before becoming Christians we disguised much of

our secret thought life, but once we became Christians, we became skilled concealers of these secret thoughts. We carefully controlled our speech and actions to keep in step with our perception of the new job description, mostly because it served our purposes. Low-awareness sins are blind spots. These low-awareness areas are where some of the most fierce battles for our minds are fought. The psalmist inquires, "Who can discern his errors? Forgive my hidden faults. Keep your servant also from willful sins; may they not rule over me. Then will I be blameless, innocent of great transgression" (Psalm 19:12–13, NIV). It's hard to beat an enemy of which we are unaware.

THE MIND THAT PLAYS TRICKS ON ITSELF

John decided to buy a new car because the gas mileage on the old one wasn't very good. The new car John bought depreciated three thousand dollars the first year, but he saved two hundred dollars in gas! What John really wanted wasn't better mileage but more prestige.

We have a remarkable capacity to kid, trick, and fool ourselves. Our self-image is so important to us that we will believe almost any reasonable explanation for our failures, as long as we end up as the hero. The prophet Jeremiah noted this when he said, "The heart is deceitful above all things and beyond cure. Who can understand it?" (Jeremiah 17:9, NIV).

Unless we develop a solid understanding of how our thoughts, motives, and ambitions are shaped, we will have impure secret thoughts, wrong motives, and selfish ambitions. If we don't leave a sentinel posted in the watchtower, then the enemy can slip into our thoughts under the cover of low awareness.

Solomon understood this when he said, "To man belong the plans of the heart, but from the LORD comes the reply of the tongue. All a man's ways seem innocent to him, but motives are weighed by the LORD" (Proverbs 16:1–2, NIV).

CONQUERING THE SECRET THOUGHT LIFE

By now you may be thinking it's hopeless to master your secret thought life. Quite to the contrary, the Holy Spirit will search our spirit and point out our errors, if we will only ask Him: "The lamp of the LORD searches the spirit of a man; it searches out his inmost being" (Proverbs 20:27, NIV). King David asked rhetorically, "Where can I go from your Spirit? Where can I flee from your presence?" (Psalm 139:7, NIV). We can run from God, but we can't hide. The answer to winning the battle for our mind—the secret thought life—is to open up ourselves to examination by ourselves and the Spirit. Our prayer should be the prayer of King David: "Search me, O God, and know my heart; test me and know my anxious thoughts. See if there is any offensive way in me, and lead me in the way everlasting" (Psalm 139:23–24, NIV).

TAKE CAPTIVE EVERY THOUGHT

Raising children is tough work. What makes it so difficult? Children always test the limits of rule and order. Whatever boundaries we set for them, they always want to test and retest the limits of our patience.

Some friends had a rule that their daughter could not go to PG-13 movies until she was thirteen. All her friends could go when they were ten and eleven. Every weekend she would ask her parents if she could go to this or that movie, always rated PG-13. She always tested the limits.

Our thoughts are like this girl. Every week they ask us to let them cross the boundaries of rule and order we have established. Our thoughts always test the limits.

What to Do?

"Take captive every thought to make it obedient to Christ" (2 Corinthians 10:5, NIV). No thought should be allowed to have its own way. Like the daughter who wants to test her parents, our thoughts want to have their own way, but we must take each and every one of them captive. Why? Because, in the words with which Solomon concluded the book of Ecclesiastes, "For God will bring every deed into judgment, including every hidden thing [our secret thought life], whether it is good or evil" (12:14, NIV).

When Christ is in control of our lives, the Holy Spirit is in power. When we let the old man—the sinful nature—be in control, then the Spirit is quenched. The solution is to bring every thought captive, and if we find we have sinned, confess it, and ask Christ to again take control. That's the essence of living by the power of the Holy Spirit.

STUDY QUESTIONS

1. Read Jeremiah 23:24. Do you believe that God knows your thoughts? Why do men put emphasis on living right among their peers, who are mere men like themselves, but do not make living right in their thought lives an equally important priority?

2. What is an area of your thought life with which you really struggle (e.g., lust, fantasies, hate-world)?

3. Read 2 Corinthians 10:5. What does it mean, "Take captive every thought"?

Taken from *The Man in the Mirror,* by Patrick M. Morley. Copyright © 1992, 1997 by Patrick Morley. Used by permission of Zondervan.

Chapter 24

Does Your Sex Drive Manage You?

By William Backus

There is a tendency to think of sex as something degrading;
it is not, it is magnificent, an enormous privilege,
but because of that the rules are tremendously strict and severe.

Francis Devas

I can still hear the pleading note in Mal's voice as he recounted for me his last conversation with his girl-friend, Ellen. They had hashed over her refusal to have sex with him for what seemed like the ninety-ninth time. "I'm a normal guy, for cryin' out loud! What am I sup-posed to do for sex?" he had demanded of her. How could she really love him and still resist him as consistently as she did? Could she be frigid?

As I listened to Mal, I thought of other men and women who have come to me seeking help with problems related to out-of-control sexuality.

There was Mark and Anita, struggling to keep themselves "pure until their wedding night"; Warren, high up in a major political party, anxious that he would not be able to perform like a sexual machine when the women he dated demanded sex; Gary, a young man who had become impotent because he feared he would not be the perfect lover; Karen, who defiantly insisted, "There's nothing wrong with having sex with someone you love"—but despised herself.

The idea of self-control was a problem for each of these single folks, trying to survive in today's permissive culture.

Nor is it any less a stumbling block for some married people. I think of Ted, whose thoughtless, self-gratifying appetites caused him nearly to rape his wife every night, causing her to hate him *and* sex; and Liz, who gave free rein to her sexual fantasies—no matter how deviant—until they drove her into affairs with fellow employees, neighbors, and even men at church. At last her embittered husband divorced her.

Clinicians encounter a veritable weed-garden of failed self-control among married people. Adulterous affairs are most common. Demands for partner participation in forms of sex that offend are common, too. Compulsive masturbation by one or the other partner may lead to avoidance of intercourse and disruption of the marital relationship. Sometimes one partner may act out in deviant sexual patterns (homosexuality, cross-dressing, exhibitionism, voyeurism, child molesting, incest), demanding in the name of love that the spouse accept the perverse behavior as harmless fun, thus becoming an enabler. Each time I hear one of these sad stories, I am impressed again with the realization that sexual "dyscontrol" can make wreckage of precious human lives.

GOD'S WAY: CHASTITY

The sexual prohibitions of God's Word weren't given to spoil man's fun, but to preserve health and sexual vitality. All these people had listened, consciously or unconsciously, both to their own sinful impulses and urges, and to the propaganda of anti-Christian thought-shapers who reiterate ad nauseam how sexual urges need not be controlled and how it is unhealthy to suppress them.

Misbeliefs in Sexual Dyscontrol

As you study the following summary of misbeliefs held by people with sexual control problems, you can use them to discover your own. There is a good chance yours will be on the list, because these false notions are seldom original. Rather, they are planted by the father of lies, who appears to be anything but creative.

Sexual Misbelief #1: I can't control my sex drive. In nearly all self-control issues, poorly controlled people tell themselves, "I can't help it!" "When I'm alone with an attractive person of the opposite sex for whom I have strong feelings, I'm gone! I can't help myself."

This misbelief actually facilitates the unwanted behavior. When you can convince yourself you are unable to help what you are about to do, you thereby *become* unable to help it. In fact, there isn't any point in struggling with an issue when the outcome is foreordained! If you can't help it, why try?

But is this old wheeze of a cliché true? The behavior you say you can't help is performed with muscles controlled voluntarily. It's not a twitch. To climb into bed you have to will certain muscles in your limbs to contract so your legs and arms bend. It is a physiological fact that you *can* exert control, that, in fact, you must *decide* to perform the actions in question. Sexual behavior doesn't happen by itself.

People who know Jesus Christ have the Holy Spirit dwelling within them and directing their actions. One result of that indwelling Spirit's work is the ability to control yourself.

If you have Jesus Christ as Savior and Lord, you *do* have the power to control your actions in sexual matters. To confess anything else is to call God a liar. Even if you think your experience teaches you otherwise, you must take the first step out of that pit—and that step is to tell yourself the truth: "I can control my actions in sexually provocative situations. Never again will I tell myself, 'I can't.'"

Sexual Misbelief #2: Chastity is bad for me. You may be telling yourself this one because you read it or heard it somewhere. It is an old notion, coming out of psychological theories devised long ago without the benefit of experimental research. If you believe this old chestnut, you have small incentive to control yourself, because you believe that control is detrimental.

Of course, this lie insinuates that God has really messed things up. Since God commands chastity and self-control in sexual matters, this misbelief actually accuses God of willing something that will harm you. God gave His best for you, and He consistently does only good. He would never order what is harmful.

Sexual Misbelief #3: Everybody else is enjoying sex immensely, so I'm left out and cheated if I control myself and they don't. It's unfair. This is merely a variation on the pervasive misbelief that when anyone else has something I don't have, God has committed a foul. It's monstrously unfair. However, we have no way of knowing for sure what's going on in another person's sex life. We can't tell what others are doing, enjoying, or feeling, so we have to rely on guesses and inferences (unless we're listening to those who brag about their supposed "conquests"). When such people tell you what they're doing, you would be wise to notice they're trying to create envy and elicit admiration.

Particularly when you know God's judgment on uncontrolled sexual behavior—namely, that those who do such things cannot inherit the kingdom of God—it makes no sense to envy the poor soul squandering eternal well-being in exchange for a few orgasms.

Sexual Misbelief #4: Others don't feel cheap and guilty about having sex, and it's unfair that I have such feelings. As for feelings of guilt, they are appropriate consequences of sinful behavior. If you feel guilt when you sin and others *say* they don't, you are the one who is better off, even if it's painful. In the same way, a person whose nervous system is intact feels the pain of injuries and is therefore much more fortunate than the person who cannot feel pain due to neurological damage. Pain, though unpleasant, is a valuable indicator of trouble and a warning to change something. Guilt feelings in consequence of truly sinful behavior signal that change is needed to avoid further spiritual and psychological damage.

Sexual Misbelief #5: Sex is just a mechanical act having no moral implications per se unless you spread disease or fail to prevent conception.

Sexual Misbelief #6: Marriage is just a formality, a mere piece of paper; it shouldn't stand in the way of people enjoying themselves. Although these two misbeliefs are shattered by the clear teachings of Scripture, there are people who argue for them, usually to justify their own sinful sexual behavior. Today, some church people declare that sexual activity outside marriage is not wrong—that while the Bible does teach that sexual intercourse should occur only between married persons of opposite sexes, this teaching is no longer appropriate. It *was* valid, long ago, because in those days contraception was not widely available and people did not know how to take precautions against venereal diseases. Today, it is argued, we have ready access to contraceptives and medications for sexually transmitted diseases, so there is no longer any reason to attach moral strictures to sexual behavior between consenting persons.

The direct result of this cultural misbelief has been an epidemic of teenage pregnancy, slaughter of the unborn in unprecedented numbers, and an enormous social burden of care for unwed mothers and their children. New sexually transmitted diseases have surfaced, some of them impossible to cure, and one invariably lethal. Unfortunately, those so glued to this cultural misbelief that no array of facts can penetrate their defenses long enough to unstick them continue prescribing more of the same "remedies" with which they compounded the social consequences of immorality in the first place: more "sex education," more "values clarification," more contraceptives, cheaper abortions, and more dollars spent for research into cures for sexually transmitted diseases. What they have not done is come forward to say, "We were wrong." Events, however, have made the point for them. The Word of God is not just another throwaway item in a throwaway culture, like yesterday's newspaper.

The truth is that each sexual act has eternal significance, bonding two individuals together in a union which, whether intended or not, exists with rather serious consequences. Read 1 Corinthians 6:15–20 for a more fulsome discussion of this bonding and its implications. For this and other very sound reasons, God is extremely serious about His commandments against impurity, fornication, sexual deviation, and adultery.

Sexual Misbelief #7: Sex is a private matter between you and your (adult) partner, and what you do in your bedroom is nobody else's business. Nothing could be further from the truth. Even though it is customary to perform sexual intercourse in private, its implications are not private. The belief that sex is a private matter has led to great difficulties for individuals and for society, including numerous families without fathers, widespread poverty, and worrisome disease epidemics for which everyone is forced to bear part of the cost. Actually, there is probably no private act with such weighty social repercussions as sexual intercourse. Because as a Christian you are responsible for the well-being of the other person, the culture, and the world, you really cannot shrug and tell yourself that what you do in the bedroom isn't anyone else's business.

Sexual Misbelief #8: A little sex never hurt anybody. What's the harm when two consenting adults do whatever they feel like doing in private? When you find yourself thinking like this, you must remind yourself of the fact that people in such situations are actually being intimate not only with an illicit partner, but with every one of that person's sexual intimates over the past years. This truth has become an issue of life and death since the AIDS plague has radically altered the meaning of casual sex, even for those who care nothing for God's commandments. A little sex cannot only hurt you, it can kill you.

STUDY QUESTIONS

1. Read 1 Corinthians 6:15–20. Do you think this type of bonding is possible in a marriage if one or both of the people involved in the relationship have had premarital sex and never repented?

2. People typically like to "push the limits" and think that they can turn back before it's too late. But with sex, that often does not happen. Have you ever asked yourself the question, "How far is too far?" Can you see an intrinsic problem with simply asking the question?

3. Have you fallen for any of these myths? If not, are there other myths that you may have fallen for? Explain.

Used by permission from *Finding the Freedom of Self-Control,* by William Backus. Copyright © 1978 by William Backus. Published by Bethany House Publishers.

Chapter 25

The Need for Purity

BY BRUCE WILKINSON

Sex is the ersatz or substitute religion of the twentieth century.

MALCOLM MUGGERIDGE

*L*odged deeply within the minds of Christian men is a most shocking thought about their sexual lives. It goes something like this: "I believe that God created man and woman, invented the powerful sex drive, and placed it within man and woman, but then He abandoned them to struggle all their lives with what to do about it. He left them helpless and trapped by a powerful sex drive with seemingly insatiable desires which can never remain satisfied for very long. I guess this part of my life can't become pleasing to God—and He must understand and overlook it as He is the one who ultimately made me the way that I am." Ever thought something like that?

The moment you read those words is the same moment you realize that something just isn't quite right. Those thoughts feel right on the surface, but they are like a knee out of joint—it doesn't bother you when you are sitting watching TV but wait until you start walking toward the kitchen on that knee—it just doesn't hold. Neither do those thoughts. Why? Because God isn't some mean, teasing, inconsistent, and uncaring despot in heaven who sets you up for failure! Then what is His solution to His creation of your sexual drives? Would it be true that if God created you with a desire for sex which reoccurs regularly, that He also has developed a corresponding strategy for its regular satisfaction and fulfillment? That would be more like the kind Lord of the Bible, wouldn't it? Well, it is. Read what He says in 1 Corinthians 7:2–5:

> But because of immoralities, let each man have his own wife, and let each woman have her own husband. Let the husband fulfill his duty to his wife, and likewise also the wife to her husband. The wife does not have authority over her own body, but the husband does; and likewise also the husband does not have authority over his own body, but the wife does. Stop depriving one another, except by agreement for a time that you may devote yourselves to prayer, and come together again lest Satan tempt you because of your lack of self-control. (NASB)

The two major problems with men in their sexual lives have to do with "sexual immorality" and "self-control." Did you notice that these three verses use the words "because of immoralities" and "because of your lack of self-control"? God's answer for both issues is the very subject of this paragraph! In fact, I believe that the Bible teaches that both issues of sexual immorality and self-control are to be solved with the same God-given solution.

What is that solution? "Let each man have his own wife, and let each woman have her own husband." The marriage relationship is God's primary provision for your sexual drives and their full expression and satisfaction. It's very interesting that both times the word *have* is used in this verse it is in the imperative. This isn't an option or a suggestion, but a command. Because of your sexual immorality, God wants you to have your own wife. Unless you have been given the gift of "singleness" which I would surmise to be an unusual gift— you are to "have" your own wife.

Now why would God say the solution to sexual immoralities (various kinds and multiple temptations) is your wife? Because, the proper fulfillment of your sex drive and your emotional love and affection is to be solidly focused in the person of your wife. When God created humans, He created both male and female, and from the beginning, God created one woman for one man. Not multiple women for one man and not men for men, but one woman for one man for life.

The moment you begin to meditate on these verses is the instant you will see the obvious answer: Fulfill your personal affections and sexual desires with your wife and she with you. Any fulfillment of your sexual needs outside of your wife is not the will of the Lord. She is the only solution. She is the God-given solution. God never intended your sex drive to be a problem but rather a pleasure to you.

That's exactly what is proclaimed in Proverbs 5:15, 18–19:

> Drink from your own cistern, and running water from your own well. Let your fountain be blessed, and rejoice with the wife of your youth. As a loving deer and a graceful doe, Let her breasts satisfy you at

all times, and always be enraptured [literally intoxi-
cated] with her love.

WHAT IS YOUR DESIRE?

Think about yesterday for a moment. How many meals did
you eat? Why did you eat them? If you are like the majority
of us, you probably ate three meals and numerous nibbles in
between—and you probably ate because you were hungry
and may have been seeking some degree of subtle comfort.

How many times did you feel guilty for feeling hungry?
You may have felt guilty about the fact that when you sat
down to eat, you crossed the barrier and overate—which the
Bible calls the sin of gluttony. But to mix the sin of gluttony
with the need and desire to eat would be a vast error! Hunger
is God-given and should be satisfied, whereas gluttony is
when a man uses that God-given need but oversteps the
acceptable boundaries of its fulfillment. You should eat to satisfy your needs but not to trespass the boundaries of normal
self-control.

Pictured in that little analogy is the identical truth applicable to your sexual life. Not only has your hunger-drive been
given by God, but so also has your sex-drive. Not only has
God provided the normal avenue to fulfill that hunger
drive—through food—but God has also provided the normal
avenue to fulfill that sex drive—through your wife.

Now, do you believe the drive for food is wrong? Do you
believe the drive for sex is wrong? Both are universal and both
are God-given. Both have universal and God-given solutions.

Let's say that for some reason, you weren't able to eat at
home when you were hungry and were forced to go without
food for days. Although you were very hungry, you felt
uncomfortable or self-conscious about asking the chef for

food. Or, when you did ask, you found the kitchen locked and unavailable to you because the chef was unwilling to cook you something to eat on that day. What would you do?

After a while, you would be severely tempted to find another source of food. Why? Because the more you didn't ask for food due to embarrassment for being hungry again, or the more you were denied food by the person who controlled it, the more your hunger would grow and push for you to seek another solution.

The only problem was that there wasn't any other lawful place to find food for yourself. The food that was rightfully yours was out of your reach, so you found yourself tempted— and soon found yourself considering food that wasn't yours.

Do you see the immediate application to what the Bible teaches? I'm utterly convinced that the vast majority of sexual immorality among Christian men is because they misunderstand the clear teachings of the Bible on this vital subject of sexual immorality. It is "because of sexual immorality" that you are to be married.

If you always had good food on the table at meal times and had little snacks here and there in the cupboard, how tempted would you be to steal other people's food and snacks? When the needs are met, the temptation to meet those needs in an appropriate manner is—for the most part—taken care of.

That's why 1 Corinthians continues with the words, "Let the husband fulfill his duty to his wife, and likewise also the wife to her husband" (7:3).

Because God has provided the "food" to meet the sexual hunger drive in each man and woman in the person of their spouse, the husband must fulfill the sexual "duty," or "obligation," to his wife and the wife to her husband.

What does the Bible mean in this context that the husband is to "fulfill his duty" except that he is to proactively be the "food" for his wife's sexual hunger? Once again the Bible doesn't leave any room for confusion in this matter because the verb *fulfill* or *render* is in the imperative—God *commands* you and your wife to meet each other's sexual needs. Are you meeting her needs? Are you having your needs met by her?

GOD'S GIFT OF SEX

What would you do if God brought your spouse to you and said, "I know that both of your sexual needs aren't being met or satisfied the way you wished—so I hereby give your wife's body to you to enjoy and to fulfill your sexual needs. I also give your body to your wife for her to enjoy and fulfill her sexual needs. I'm taking your authority away from you over your own body—because you are living like you owned your body and only give it to each other begrudgingly or too seldom. Whenever you desire sex, you have the full rights and privileges of full authority over your spouse's body to fulfill those needs and wishes."

Your mouth would probably drop open in disbelief. If God continued, "I only have two additional comments. First, whenever your partner comes to you for sexual affection, you must treat the other person with consideration, kindness, gentleness, and love. Second, since I have created you with strong and regular desires for sex, please feel free to have sex as often as you desire it. When you have sexual temptations, make sure you fulfill them with each other—and enjoy the pleasure that I have intricately linked to sexual intimacy—it's one of My most special gifts to you." How would you feel? And, if your spouse's body became yours to enjoy within the boundaries of affection, would you do anything differently?

What the Bible Teaches

Guess what? God read your mind, knows your drives, and literally gave you the body of your spouse! When you said those marital vows, the authority of your body was given to her and her body was given to you.

Who would have ever known that God felt so strongly about the sexual intimacy issue? Who would have ever dreamt that God felt so strongly about our sexual drives that He literally gave us "authority" over our spouse's body? Why would God go to such an extreme except to fully provide an acceptable and proper and pleasing solution for a drive He created?

Are you obeying the will of God?

Sexual Needs in Marriage

One of the foundational beliefs that I hold is that the Bible is the absolute and utterly reliable Truth from God. Its answers are true answers regardless of what I may think. When my thoughts agree with the Bible, I'm in safe territory, but when my thoughts or behavior do not agree with the Bible, I'm in dangerous territory. Take this subject, for instance: If you asked the average modern man what the main solution is for sexual immorality, what would he say? I have looked through innumerable books on the subject and it's the rare book that presents the clear biblical solution to sexual immorality to be for the marriage partners to enjoy sex as often as they desire, including the rights to their spouse's body to fulfill those needs.

How often should you turn down you spouse's sexual advances and she turn down yours? The Bible shouts the answer: "Stop depriving one another!" That can also be translated, "Stop robbing each other." James 5:4 best clarifies the meaning: "Indeed the wages of the laborers who mowed your fields, which you kept back by *fraud* cry out; and the cries of the reapers have reached the ears of the Lord of the Sabaoth." Because the Lord has given you the body of your spouse to meet your ongoing sexual needs, then for your wife to withhold her body from you is actually to steal something that is not hers! Likewise, when we say no to our wife's sexual needs, we rob her of something that God Himself has given her.

Following the general principle of "stop depriving one another," the Bible outlines three exceptions: First, you can deprive each other by "agreement." This means that if you both agree not to have sexual relations, then not having them is acceptable to the Lord. Therefore, it is fully acceptable to request a postponement from the other person but not acceptable to deny the other person if they don't agree.

Second, you can deprive each other only "for a time," which sets a time limit on how long the postponement can be. Obviously, the postponement is "by agreement for a time" and requires both partners to consent to a mutually acceptable time.

Third, the only revealed reason in this passage to ask permission to "deprive one another" is for both of you to devote your full attention to spiritual matters including prayer and fasting. Note that the words "that you may devote yourselves to prayer" is in the plural—that both you and your wife are involved in this "sexual fast" for spiritual purposes.

Last, you should "come together again lest Satan tempt you because of your lack of self-control." These words are packed with rich insight about sexual realities. Did you see that the Bible openly teaches that by not having regular sexual relations, your self-control will definitely be affected? For example, you may be bothered a little if you skip a meal, or even fast for a day, but if you continue to be denied food, you will "fight" hunger drives more and more intensely. Similarly, if one partner decides to defraud the other of sexual relations, they are actually forcing their spouse to fight Satanic temptations that he or she would otherwise not have to face! This verse doesn't say "lest Satan may tempt" or "may occasionally tempt" but "lest Satan tempt."

What's the point? Do you know anyone who you think may need to have a long and intimate conversation with his spouse about these very issues?

STUDY QUESTIONS

1. Why do you think so many men feel ashamed or reluctant to let their wives know how often they want to have sex? What would your wife say if you were completely transparent with her?

2. If the average Christian man had sex as often as he needed it in his marriage, how much do you think it would help his struggle with temptation?

3. What principles for godly sexuality can you glean from 1 Corinthians 7?

Used by permission from the *Personal Holiness in Times of Temptation* video course workbook, by Dr. Bruce H. Wilkinson. Copyright © 1997 by Bruce Wilkinson and Walk Thru the Bible.

Chapter 26

Closing the Door to Lust

By Charles Swindoll

There is little praise for the consistently sexually controlled single. Too often, it is mixed with granulated pity or powdered condescension. Ironically, while discipline and self-control are encouraged and admired in scholarship, athletics, music, and ministry, their absence is strangely excused in sexual matters. The secular myth has infiltrated the Christian consciousness; our sexual urges are overpowering and irresistible.... Chastity is a requisite of Christian singleness. Furthermore, chastity is possible. There will always be somebody to suggest that such thinking is legalistic, unreasonable, and unlikely to succeed. My reply can only be: "When it's bigger than I am, so is God."

ROSALIE DE ROSSET

Samson was a he-man with a she-weakness. In spite of the fact that he was born of godly parents, set apart from his birth to be a Nazarite, and elevated to the enviable position of judge in Israel, he never conquered his tendency toward lust. On the contrary, it conquered him. Several things that illustrate his lustful bent may be observed from the record of his life in the book of Judges.

1. The first recorded words from his mouth were, "I saw a woman" (14:2, NASB).

2. He was attracted to the opposite sex strictly on the basis of outward appearance: "Get her for me, for she looks good to me" (14:3, NASB).

3. He judged Israel for twenty years, then went right back to his old habit of chasing women: a harlot in Gaza, and finally Delilah (15:20–16:4).

4. He became so preoccupied with his lustful desires, he didn't even know the Lord had departed from him (16:20).

THE CONSEQUENCES OF LUST

The results of Samson's illicit affairs are familiar to all of us. The strongman of Dan was taken captive and became a slave in the enemy's camp, his eyes were gouged out of his head, and he was appointed to be the grinder in a Philistine prison. Lust, the jailer, binds and blinds and grinds. The swarthy pride of Israel, who once held the highest office in the land, was now the bald-headed clown of Philistia—a pathetic, hollow shell of humanity. His eyes would never wander again. His life, once filled with promise and dignity, was now a portrait of hopeless, helpless despair. Chalk up another victim for lust. The perfumed memories of erotic pleasure in Timnah, Gaza, and the infamous Valley of Sorek were now overwhelmed by the putrid stench of a Philistine dungeon.

Without realizing it, Solomon wrote another epitaph—this one for Samson's tombstone:

> The wicked man is doomed by his own sins; they are ropes that catch and hold him. He shall die because he will not listen to the truth; he has let himself be led away into incredible folly. (Proverbs 5:22–23, TLB)

The same words could well be chiseled in the marble over many other tombs. I think, for example, of the silver-throated orator of Rome, Mark Antony. In his early manhood, he was so consumed with lust that his tutor once shouted in disgust: "O Marcus! O colossal child…able to conquer the world, but unable to resist a temptation!"

CHRISTIANS UNDER ATTACK

I think of the gentleman I met several years ago—a fine itinerant Bible teacher. He said he had been keeping a confidential list of men who were once outstanding expositors of the Scripture. Capable and respected men of God…who have shipwrecked their faith on the shoals of moral defilement. During the previous week, he said, he had entered the name of *number 42* in his book. This sad, sordid statistic, he claims, caused him to be extra cautious and discreet in his own life. Perhaps by now he has added a couple dozen more names.

A chill ran down my spine when he told that story. No one is immune. You're not. I'm not. Lust is no respecter of persons. Whether by savage assault or subtle suggestion, the minds of a wide range of people are vulnerable to its attack: sharp professional men and women, homemakers, students, carpenters, artists, musicians, pilots, bankers, senators, plumbers, promoters, and preachers as well. Its alluring voice can infiltrate the most intelligent mind and cause its victim to believe its lies and respond to its appeal.

And beware: It never gives up; it never runs out of ideas. Bolt your front door, and it will rattle at the bedroom window, crawl into the living room through the TV screen, or wink at you out of a magazine in the den.

CHRIST AS YOUR MESSENGER

How do you handle such an aggressive intruder? Try this: When lust suggests a rendezvous, send Jesus Christ as your representative.

Have Him inform your unwanted suitor that you want nothing to do with illicit desire—nothing. Have your Lord remind lust that since you and Christ have been united together, you are no longer a slave to sin. His death and resurrection freed you from sin's stranglehold and gave you a new Master. And before giving lust a firm shove away from your life, have Christ inform this intruder that the permanent peace and pleasure you are enjoying in your new home with Christ are so much greater than lust's temporary excitement that you don't need it around any longer to keep you happy.

> For sin's power over us was broken when we became Christians and were baptized to become a part of Jesus Christ; through His death the power of your sinful nature was shattered. Your old sin-loving nature was buried with Him by baptism when He died, and when God the Father, with glorious power, brought Him back to life again, you were given His wonderful new life to enjoy. (Romans 6:3–4, TLB)

But lust is persistent. If it has knocked on your door once, it will knock again. And again. You are safe just so long as you draw upon your Savior's strength. Try to handle it yourself and you'll lose—every time. This is why we are warned again and again in the New Testament *to flee* sexual temptations. Remember, lust is committed to wage war against your soul—in a life-and-death struggle, in hand-to-hand combat. Don't stand before this mortal enemy and argue or fight in your own strength. Run for cover. Cry out for reinforcement. Call in an air strike. If you get yourself into a situation that leaves you defenseless and weak, if your door is left even slightly ajar, you may be sure that this ancient enemy will kick it open with six-guns blazing. So don't leave it open. Don't give lust a foothold...or even a toehold.

THE EXAMPLE OF JOSEPH

Joseph was a dedicated, well-disciplined believer, but he was smart enough to realize he couldn't tease lust without being whipped (read Genesis 39). When it came time for a hasty exit, the son of Jacob preferred to leave his jacket behind rather than hesitate and leave his hide.

But not Samson. Fool that he was, he thought he could cuddle lust, inhale its heady perfume, and enjoy its warm embrace without the slightest chance of getting caught. What appeared to be a harmless, soft, attractive dove of secret love turned into a reeking nightmarish vulture.

Lust is one flame you dare not fan. You'll get burned if you do.

Samson would sign this warning in my place if he could, for he, being dead, yet speaks.

STUDY QUESTIONS

1. Search through 1 Thessalonians 4:1–12 and find at least three guidelines for how to close your door to lust. Write them down on a card and keep it available.

2. What can you learn from Samson about giving in to sexual temptation?

3. What can you learn from Joseph about not giving in to sexual temptation?

Taken from *Come Before Winter and Share My Hope*, by Charles R. Swindoll. Copyright © 1985 by Charles R. Swindoll. Used by permission of Zondervan.

Chapter 27

Strategies to Keep
from Falling

By Randy Alcorn

It is with our passions, as it is with fire and water.
They are good servants but bad masters.

Sir Roger l'Estrange

Something terrible has happened." The tense voice was my friend's, calling from across the country. "Yesterday our pastor left his wife and ran off with another woman."

I was sad, but not shocked or even surprised. Twenty-five years ago, I would have been shocked. Fifteen years ago I would have been surprised. But I've heard the same story too many times now to ever be surprised again.

I spoke on sexual purity at a Bible college. During that week, many students came for counseling, including three I'll call Rachel, Barb, and Pam.

Rachel got right to the point: "My parents sent me to one of our pastors for counseling, and I ended up sleeping with him." Later the same day, Barb, a church leader's daughter, told me through tears, "My dad has had sex with me for years, and now he's starting on my sisters." The next evening I met with Pam. Her story? "I came to Bible college to get away from an affair with my pastor."

For every well-known Christian television personality or author whose impropriety is widely publicized, there are any number of lesser-known pastors, Bible teachers, and parachurch workers who quietly resign or are fired for sexual immorality. Most of us can name several. The myth that ministers are morally invulnerable dies slowly, however, even in the face of overwhelming evidence. But there never has been a mystical antibody that makes us immune to sexual sin. Even those of us who haven't fallen know how fierce is the struggle with temptation.

I recall with embarrassment my naïveté as a young pastor. Every time I heard the stories of Christian leaders falling into sexual sin, I thought, *It could never happen to me.*

What level of pride is required to believe that sexual sin could overtake Samson, David ("a man after God's own heart"), Solomon, and a host of modern Christian leaders, but not *me?* Paul's warning in 1 Corinthians 10:12 (NIV) deserves a prominent place on our dashboards, desks, or Day-Timers: "If you think you are standing firm, be careful that you don't fall!"

Fortunately, I wised up. The person who believes he will never be burglarized leaves his doors and windows open, and cash on the top of his dresser. Likewise, the one who thinks the danger isn't real invariably takes risks that wind up proving costly. I now live with the frightening but powerfully motivating knowledge that *I could* commit sexual immorality. I started taking precautions to keep it from happening to me.

PRACTICAL GUIDELINES FOR SEXUAL PURITY

Monitoring my spiritual pulse. Often those who fall into sexual sin can point back to lapses in their practices of meditation, worship, prayer, and the healthy self-examination such disciplines foster. All of us know this, but in the busyness of giving out help, we can easily neglect the replenishing of our spiritual reservoirs.

Daily disciplines are important, of course, but I've found that for me they're not enough. God gave Israel not merely one hour a day but one day a week, several weeks a year, and even one year every seven to break the pattern of life long enough to worship and reflect and take stock.

I periodically take overnight retreats by myself or with my wife. In times of greater need, I've been away a week, usually in a cabin on the Oregon coast. This is not a vacation, but a time in which the lack of immediate demands and the absence of noise give clarity to the still, small voice of God that is too easily drowned in the busyness of my daily life.

GUARDING MY MARRIAGE

I find I must regularly evaluate my relationship with my wife. In particular, I watch for the red flags of discontentment, poor communication, and poor sexual relationship. We try to spend regular, uninterrupted time together to renew our spiritual, intellectual, emotional, and physical closeness.

Many Christian leaders move so freely and deeply in the world of great spiritual truths and activities that, unless they take pains to communicate daily, their spouses get left out. This development of two separate worlds leads to two separate lives and is often the first step toward an adulterous affair with "someone who understands me and my world."

Communication is key because every adultery begins

with a deception, and most deceptions begin with seemingly innocent secrets—things "she doesn't need to know."

At work, I surround myself with reminders of my spouse and children: pictures and mementos. When traveling, I make contact with my wife as often as possible. If I'm struggling with temptation, I try to be honest and ask for prayer. Fierce loyalty to our wives is also a key. I try always to speak highly of my wife in public and never to downgrade her to others. And I'm careful not to discuss my marriage problems with anyone of the opposite sex.

TAKING PRECAUTIONS

One pastor found his thoughts were continually drawn to a coworker, more than to his own wife. After months of rationalizing, he finally admitted to himself that he was looking for reasons to spend time with her. Then his rule of thumb became: I will meet with her only when necessary, only as long as necessary, only at the office, and with others present as much as possible. In time, his relationship with her returned to its original, healthy coworker status.

The questions with which I check myself: Do I look forward in a special way to my appointments with this person? Would I rather see her than my wife? Do I seek to meet with her away from my office in a more casual environment? Do I prefer that my coworkers not know I'm meeting with her again? An affirmative answer to any of these questions is, for me, a warning light.

DEALING WITH THE SUBTLE SIGNS OF SEXUAL ATTRACTION

A relationship can be sexual long before it becomes erotic. Just because I'm not touching a woman, or just because I'm not envisioning specific erotic encounters, does not mean I'm not becoming sexually involved with her. The erotic is usually not the beginning but the culmination of sexual attraction. Most pastors who end up in bed with a woman do it not just to gratify a sexual urge, but because they believe they've begun to really love her.

I once casually asked a woman about her obvious interest in a married man with whom she worked. "We're just friends," she responded with a defensiveness that indicated they weren't. "It's purely platonic, nothing sexual at all." In a matter of months, however, the two friends found themselves sneaking off from their families to be with each other, and finally their "friendship" developed into an affair that destroyed both of their marriages.

Lust isn't just unbridled passion. Even when it's "bridled," it may lead us down a path that our conscience could not have condoned had we experienced it in a more obvious, wanton way. Thus, our enemies are not only lascivious thoughts of sex, but "innocuous" feelings of infatuation as well.

CLEARING CLOUDY THOUGHTS

Often we justify our flirtations with logical, even spiritual, rationalizations. One pastor didn't tell his wife about his frequent meetings with a particular woman on the grounds he shouldn't violate confidentialities, even to his wife. Besides, he sensed his wife would be jealous (without good reason, of course), so why upset her? Under the cloak of professionalism and sensitivity to his wife, he proceeded to meet with this woman secretly. The result was predictable.

Another pastor had been struggling with lustful thoughts toward a college girl in his church. Rather than dealing with his struggles alone with the Lord, with a mature brother, or with his wife, he took the girl out to lunch to talk with her. Citing the biblical mandate to confess our sins and make things right with the person we've wronged, he told her, "I've been having lustful thoughts about you, and I felt I needed to confess them to you." Embarrassed but flattered, the girl began to entertain her own thoughts toward him, and finally they became sexually involved.

All this came from what the pastor told himself was a spiritual and obedient decision to meet with the girl. To misuse Scripture in this way and violate rules of wisdom and common sense shows how cloudy and undependable our thinking can become.

GUARDING MY MIND

A battering ram may hit a fortress gate a thousand times, and no one time seems to have an effect. Yet finally the gate caves in. Likewise, immorality is the cumulative product of small mental indulgences and minuscule compromises, the immediate consequences of which were, at the time, indiscernible.

Our thoughts are the fabric with which we weave our character and destiny. No, we can't avoid all sexual stimuli, but "if you're on a diet, don't go into a doughnut shop." For me this means such practical things as staying away from the magazine racks, video stores, advertisements, programs, Internet sites, images, people, and places that tempt me to lust.

One man who travels extensively told me about a practice that has helped to guard his mind from immorality. "Whenever I check into my hotel," he said, "where I normally stay for three or four days, I ask them at the front desk to please remove the television from my room. Invariably, they look at me like I'm crazy, and then they say; 'But, sir, if you don't want to watch it, you don't have to turn it on.' Since I'm a paying customer, however, I politely insist, and I've never once been refused."

REGULARLY REHEARSING THE CONSEQUENCES

I met with a man who had been a leader in a Christian organization until he fell into immorality. I asked him, "What could have been done to prevent this?"

He paused for only a moment, then said with haunting pain and precision, "If only I had really known, really thought through what it would cost me and my family and my Lord, I honestly believe I never would have done it."

In the wake of several Christian leaders falling into immorality, a pastor and I developed a list of specific consequences that would result from our immorality (posted at our website, www.epm.org/leadpur2.html). The list was devastating, and to us it spoke more powerfully than any sermon or article on the subject.

Periodically, especially when traveling or in a time of weakness, we read through the list. In a tangible and personal way, it brings home God's inviolate law of choice and consequence, cutting through the fog of rationalization and filling our hearts with the healthy, motivating fear of God.

WINNING THE BATTLE

In J. R. R. Tolkien's book *The Hobbit,* there was no one seemingly more invincible than Smaug, the mighty dragon. But then that unlikely hero, Bilbo Baggins, found one small weak spot in Smaug's underbelly. That information, in the hands of a skilled marksman, was all it took to seal the doom of the presumptuous dragon. Unaware of his weakness and underestimating his opponents, Smaug failed to protect himself. An arrow pierced his heart, and the dragon was felled.

An exciting story with a happy ending. But when it's a Christian leader felled, the ending is not so happy. It's tragic. The evil one knows only too well the weak spots of the most mighty Christian warriors, not to mention the rest of us. He isn't one to waste his arrows, bouncing them harmlessly off the strongest plates of our spiritual armor. His aim is deadly, and it is at our points of greatest vulnerability that he will most certainly attack.

We are in a battle—a battle far more fierce and strategic than any that Alexander, Hannibal, or Napoleon ever fought. We must realize that no one prepares for a battle of which he is unaware, and no ones wins a battle for which he doesn't prepare.

STUDY QUESTIONS

1. A man's ego is often bolstered by the encouragements of a beautiful woman, often leading to sexual sin. What steps can you take now to prevent this problem from occurring in your life?

2. What is one step you can consistently take to guard your mind from sexual temptation? Are there other steps you can commit to take?

3. If you were to get involved in an adulterous affair, what would the consequences be? Take some time to sit down and write out every consequence you can think of. Then fold the list and put it in your wallet. Take it out every now and then and review it.

Chapter 28

"But I Can't Let Her Go"

By Erwin Lutzer

*To read the papers and the magazines you would
think we were almost worshiping the female bosom.*

BILLY GRAHAM

His final words caught my attention. They came at the end of a long discussion with a married man about his concealed affair with a woman he truly loved. He said the words slowly and deliberately: "I can't let her go."

Being unable to let go also applies to other sins, but breaking a relationship with another human being is more difficult. There has been a sharing of intimacies. Abstinence seems unrealistic to one who has known fulfillment.

For you to suggest otherwise brings the objection, "You don't understand!"

Yet God says these desires are to be laid to rest. He knows we are not at the mercy of our feelings. We read: "No temptation has overtaken you but such as is common to man; and God is faithful, who will not allow you to be tempted beyond what you are able, but with the temptation will provide the way of escape also, that you may be able to endure it" (1 Corinthians 10:13, NASB).

Consider also Christ's startling statement: "Everyone who looks on a woman to lust for her has committed adultery with her already in his heart." (Matthew 5:28, NASB). With such a high standard, all are indicted.

How can such desires be brought under control? Christ anticipated our response. He knows that parting with lust is like getting rid of a part of our bodies.

So He continued:

> And if your right eye makes you stumble, tear it out, and throw it from you; for it is better for you that one of the parts of your body perish, than for your whole body to be thrown into hell. And if your right hand makes you stumble, cut it off, and throw it from you; for it is better for you that one of the parts of your body perish, than for your whole body to go into hell (Matthew 5:29–30, NASB).

The term *stumbling block* refers to a bait stick in a trap. The picture is that of a pit covered with a thin layer of branches for the unwary traveler to step on and fall in. Christ is saying that if your eye or hand causes you to be tripped up with sexual temptation, take drastic action.

He said that if it is necessary to cut off a hand or pluck out an eye to keep sexually pure, do it! Unfortunately, His words are often dismissed because it's argued He was speaking figuratively.

Though Christ wasn't telling us to amputate parts of our bodies, He expects us to cut off the source of our lust or to remove ourselves from the temptation.

AMPUTATION IS PAINFUL

Sitting in my study, I'm trying to visualize my right arm amputated. In ancient times there was no anesthetic to alleviate the throbbing torment that would accompany surgery. Afterward, grotesque scars would remain. But with the diseased limb removed, there was hope for recovery.

Christ knew we wouldn't part with our hands and eyes unless it was absolutely necessary. We would do anything to spare them. Lust is as difficult to part with. Anyone who has experienced the exhilaration of sexual attraction knows that.

Recently, I spoke to a man who was in love with another woman, but they had decided to break off their relationship so he could go back to his wife and family and rebuild his marriage. He still had a deep affection for the woman, and he wondered why his emotions didn't change toward his wife.

Just as when a marriage partner dies, a healing process must take place. There will be grief, tears, and loneliness. Yet Christ says, "Do it."

How? First, by getting away from the temptation. Paul's advice is to "flee immorality" (1 Corinthians 6:18, NASB); "flee from youthful lusts" (2 Timothy 2:22, NASB). Run from temptation without leaving a forwarding address.

What if temptation is close—next door or at the job? The seed of sensuality must be crushed before it gets an opportunity to become firmly rooted in mind and body. Whatever it takes, stop it.

It may be necessary to change jobs, stop visiting certain places, or part company with friends who influence you to do evil (Proverbs 1:10–19).

It's true this won't guarantee immunity from further enticement, but that doesn't negate Christ's words. Often Christians know precisely what they could do to counteract sin's inroads.

We must ask God to "lead us not into temptation" (Matthew 6:13, KJV). Daily we are confronted with sin in a hundred different disguises. But God can keep us from stumbling. "The Lord knows how to rescue the godly from temptation" (2 Peter 2:9, NASB).

We must fling the stumbling block aside, treating it as we would a mugger. It is not the time for negotiations and a drawn-out farewell.

Saying no to our passions is painful but possible. Many have had an arm amputated when gangrene has set in. They endured the suffering to contain the poison.

Christ knew it wouldn't be easy. Yet He asked us to do it for our own good and for His name's sake.

AMPUTATION IS THOROUGH

Suppose you go to a surgeon with a cancerous growth on your arm and he says, "I plan to do this in stages; I'll cut out most of it this time and take more later. We won't decide now whether we eventually will take it all."

That's absurd. You want him to make sure he's got it all the first time.

This should also be true of sexual sin. Puritan writer Benjamin Needler put it this way: "We must not part with sin, as with a friend, with a purpose to see it again and to have the same familiarity with it as before, or possibly greater.... We must shake our hands of it as Paul did shake the viper off his hand into the fire."

We are to burn every bridge behind us—no turning back. Just as the ancient Jews searched their houses with a candle to be sure there was no leaven left among them, we must diligently search our lives lest there be a bit of sin left to deaden our lives.

I don't mean just sexual sin; any sin we tolerate can be the cause of failure in sexual temptations. Paul taught that immorality, impurity, sensuality, idolatry, sorcery, and other sensual sins have a common root: the flesh (see Galatians 5:19–21).

Compromise in one matter leads to problems in another. Unresolved anger can lead to drunkenness, dishonesty to immorality.

In Joshua 7, Israel was routed when fighting the men of Ai. A military expert would have evaluated the army, studied its tactics, and recommended better strategy and equipment. But the real cause of Israel's defeat was that Achan had stolen a garment that was to have been destroyed along with the city of Jericho. On the surface they were unrelated, but God established the connection.

Because all sin has the common root of rebellion, one sin, however distantly related, can be the cause of another. The forces that open the heart's door to lust may be fed from a different source.

You might not think cheating on your income tax can lead to failing in sexual temptation, but it can. If covetousness caused a military defeat, it can cause a moral one as well.

A. W. Tozer wrote, "The part of ourselves that we rescue from the cross may be a very little part of us, but it is likely to be the seat of our spiritual troubles and our defeats."

Take an unhurried half hour and pray with the psalmist, "Search me, O God, and know my heart; try me and know my anxious thoughts; and see if there be any hurtful way in me, and lead me in the everlasting way" (Psalm 139:23–24, NASB).

AMPUTATION IS WORTHWHILE

Is the pain worth it? Ask the cancer patient who has been told by his surgeon, "We got it all."

But this exhilaration fades in comparison with the advantages of moral freedom. Christ said that if one is faced with losing his eye or losing his soul, it would be foolish to keep the eye.

To ruin the soul through guilt and shame (even if we'll be saved as if by fire) is a high price to pay for forbidden pleasure.

A man with only one hand and one eye is unable to fulfill his cherished dreams. He has no option except to redirect his life toward simpler goals.

Christ knows our disappointments. Yet He says it's better to be able to claim God's friendship than to be fulfilled and incur God's disfavor. God is a friend of the lonely, frustrated, and tempted, but He will judge those who commit immorality (Hebrews 13:4).

Walter Trobisch spoke with insight: "The task we have to face is the same, whether we are married or single: to live a fulfilled life in spite of many unfulfilled desires."

Sexual sin, however appealing, is never worth more than an arm or a leg. Someone has said, "How prompt we are to satisfy the hunger and thirst of our bodies; how slow to satisfy the hunger and thirst of our souls."

You can only jump over a chasm in one long jump, not two short ones. We need to obey instantly—whatever the cost.

BREAKING THE RELATIONSHIP

Let's return to the case of the man who says, "I can't let her go."

God has said no to their relationship. But they have given themselves to an intimate relationship and have developed a feeling of indebtedness. The woman may say to him, "If you leave me, I'll commit suicide." Or she may say, "If you leave me,

I'll spread it all over town. You've got more to lose than I do."

What can the man do? He can approach her in a spirit of humility and confess his part of the sin. It's useless to argue who is responsible—to a degree, both of them are.

He should help her to see he is genuinely sorry he robbed her of intimacy—that he stole what he did not own and that he took a path that leads to destruction.

He can tell her this is the end. It's final. He should be willing to submit to any discipline the Lord might allow. Fear of exposure must not prevent confessing and forsaking sin. The detour is always rougher than the main road.

No one has succeeded in making the way of the transgressor easy. But whatever happens, it will likely be less serious than losing an eye or a hand.

Yes, he can let her go.

STUDY QUESTIONS

1. Is there a person, place, or thing in your life that continually causes you to stumble sexually? According to Matthew 5:29–30, what is the best way to deal with it?

2. What is more important to you: immoral sex or your relationship with God? Do you think one can keep you from the other?

3. Has God so abandoned any Christian that he is justified in saying, "I can't let go of my sexual sin"?

Taken from *Living with Your Passions,* by Erwin Lutzer, Copyright © 1983. Used by permission of the author.

Chapter 29

The Hidden Power
of Friends

By Gary Smalley and John Trent, Ph.D.

*No man is an island, entire of itself;
every man is a piece of the continent, a part of the main.*

John Donne

*A*ll of us face storms in life, but not everyone has a shelter from the storm. Thankfully, Kyle and Ann did. And if that shelter hadn't been there for them to run to, their marriage and family would have been shattered on the rocks.

Kyle and Ann live in a typical home in a typical suburb in southern California. They have two children, two cars, and the typical struggles that every couple faces. But what isn't typical is something Kyle and Ann committed themselves to several years ago that saved their marriage.

For fifteen years, Kyle and Ann had weathered life's storms together. At times, their problems were like gale-force winds, but their marriage had never come close to capsizing—that is, until recently.

In the midst of financial and extended family problems, Kyle finally felt he had reached the breaking point. Tired of the storm winds and of being driven emotionally night and day, in a tirade, he decided the only option left to him was to desert his wife and family.

Kyle tried to jump ship, but tied around his life was a line of support and accountability that kept him from going under, and his family from running aground.

Without realizing it, Kyle and Ann had made one of the most important decisions of their married life when they joined a support group of other couples. Over the months, they had strengthened their support lines to the point that when Kyle began packing, Ann went to the phone and immediately called Terry, another man in the group. Within minutes, Terry had called Mike, yet another man in their group.

Like a 9-1-1 alert, the message went out that Kyle and Ann were in trouble. And after a response time that would make any fire chief proud, Kyle was staring at his two friends.

For months, these men had met weekly, usually on Saturday morning at 6:00 A.M., sharing each other's burdens, talking about financial woes or marital frictions. On any given Saturday, they might be going through a book together, or one man might have a particular verse to share. But always there was time to pray for each other, to listen, to encourage.

And while they didn't have it written down, in unwritten words their small group provided two essential ingredients that would prove the difference between Kyle and Ann's falling apart or staying together.

First, Terry drove over and talked to Kyle, offering the emotional support of a close friend. Later, Kyle said that his time with Terry was like having an ice pack and a splint applied to a wrenched ankle. Shortly after that, Mike arrived, providing another dose of encouragement and support.

Since they were both joggers, Mike suggested, "Let's talk while we're running around the block." And as Kyle let out built-up physical steam in their four trips around the block, even more importantly, he let go of the dam of emotional pressure that had built up in his life.

His time with Mike was a period of repentance, cleansing, and healing. As they walked and ran together, Kyle finally broke down and began to cry. For the first time in years, he let down all his burdens.

That's what it can mean to be part of a small group—having a friend to stand beside you, to put his arm around you when you're weeping; to provide comfort and conversation that lead you to a decision you knew all along was right; to stay with your family and work things out; and in the weeks to come, someone to walk with as you're healing.

While Terry and Mike supported Kyle, their wives, Gail and Shirley, were there for Ann. And the result was that instead of becoming another single-parent home in the sea of heartache, Kyle and Ann became a shelter from the storm. A place of repair. And a safe place for children to grow up without fear of sinking ships.

The two keys that held Kyle to his family were the lifelines of *support* and *accountability* within their small group. But how many other Kyles and Anns ended up jumping overboard that day, thinking it would be easier just to swim to a new start, only to be caught in riptides of emotional pain that could drag them under?

From the time Jesus left us to live out the Christian life, He put us in groups—small centers of support, yet ones that are big enough to give us the help we desperately need during times of trouble, and major encouragement for positive growth.

SMALL GROUP GIVES LOVING SUPPORT

What do we mean specifically when we write of gaining "support"? And why is it such an important benefit today?

Actually, the support of men for other men is ages old. In the Old Testament, we see a dramatic story of how, without the support of a few friends, a great battle would have been lost.

Under the command of Joshua, the army of Israel fought bravely against the Amalekites. But victory was far from certain. Whether or not Israel would prevail depended on a miracle.

From his vantage point on top of a hill, Moses saw that as long as he held up the staff of God in his hands, Israel was winning the battle. But when he lowered his hands, the tide turned in favor of the Amalekites. So Moses bravely stood and held up the staff.

It was inevitable, however, that his strength would begin to wane…his arms to drop slowly…and Israel would go down to defeat. But that didn't happen. Why? One word: *support*.

Aaron stood on one side of Moses, helping him hold up one hand. And Hur stood on the other side, supporting his other hand. The result was a great victory for Israel that day.

That's exactly what we're calling men to do with men today—to stand next to a brother who's committed to holding up his sword in the battle for his family. And should his strength ever subside, he's got someone right there to help him hold up his sword and win the victory.

With all the pressures and trials we face, it's hard to stand alone. And the fact is, we don't have to. Scripture tells us that if one can make a thousand flee, two can make ten thousand flee! There is power in linking up with a group that can help us be the men we're called to be.

A Higher Motivation to Do What's Right

Have you ever suffered from a lack of motivation? Not just the desire to pull the covers back over your head when the alarm goes off on a cold winter's morning, but the lack of inner resolve to deal with a small problem before it becomes a large one. To make that father-daughter date you've talked about a reality, not just a goal. To finally confront your father in an honest, loving way—face-to-face, not just in your dreams. Or to follow through on so many good ideas you've heard at conferences or at church, but somehow you have left in a notebook or forgotten on the walk to your car.

Another important benefit of a small group is the every-week encouragement to do your best and *be* your best. It's the accountability you get when a support person asks a simple question like "How's it going this week?" or "What happened when you did your homework?" or "What's one way you could solve that problem this week?" It's great to have a personal cheerleading squad—people who are going to appreciate your efforts and reward them with a "Well done!" People pulling for you to make it, not blow it. People who will say, "That's great!" and clap and cheer when you make progress. But a *super* motivational charge comes when loving people ask if you did last week what you promised to do.

For some men, particularly those who have suffered a difficult past, internal motivation is hard to drum up. In fact, one secular bestselling book captures this problem in its title: *Passive Men and Wild Women!* The author puts his finger on a common problem across our country: namely, a number of men tend to be more passive or slower in developing good relationships than their spouses. The loving support and *accountability* of a small group is a major part of the solution.

When a man struggles to take an active role in family

decisions, to be the spiritual leader in the home, to get involved in the lives of his children, or even to work at putting bread on the table, pressure can build to the breaking point in a home. Often without realizing it, his inactivity has become a purposeful choice. If he sits still long enough (usually just as Dad did), the pressure will finally catapult his wife into a frenzy of activity, and she'll do the job he's supposed to handle.

Soon, instead of a marriage team, you've got only one player on the field, and she's exhausted! The more passive the man gets, the wilder she becomes, and the worse the model they both provide to the children, who don't miss a moment of the battle.

Men, it may be a hard pill to swallow, but laziness is a learned activity. Even for committed procrastinators, however, there is hope. Without exception, the men we've seen in counseling who struggle with a lack of motivation *are not in small groups*. But we've seen time and again that when men finally join a healthy group, things begin to change. Why? Because of that same powerful one-two punch of loving support and healthy accountability that brings things in the darkness into the light.

GAIN SELF-CONTROL OVER UNWANTED HABITS AND THOUGHTS

There's nothing more powerful than a deep inner sense of self-control. And it's a power you can develop in a small, supportive group.

- It's the strength to keep your tongue still at work when everyone else is ripping the boss to shreds behind his back.
- It's the resolve to turn past the "adults-only" movie channel in the hotel room, even when you're all alone and it's late at night.

- It's the courage to count to ten…and then to ten again…instead of ripping into your spouse or teenagers when they irritate you.

In Proverbs 16:32 (NASB), we read that "he who is slow to anger is better than the mighty, and he who rules his spirit, than he who captures a city."

Ruling your spirit. Keeping tabs on your temper. Slowing down your reactions so you behave responsibly instead of selfishly. These are earmarks of self-control, true masculinity.

Whether you're hooked on cable-television channels, sexual temptation, out-of-control spending, overeating, or substance abuse—whether you're caught up in the first steps of any addiction or twenty miles down the road to ruin—you've got hope! At least you do if you've got a small group of close friends to give you that support and accountability.

STUDY QUESTIONS

1. There are four character traits that need to be present in a person who is accountable: vulnerability, teachability, honesty, and availability. What do each of these mean to you? Are there any that you're lacking?

2. Can you think of anyone to whom you're accountable? Of what benefit is this accountability?

3. Take a moment and write down the names of one or two people you could be accountability partners with. After talking with them, set up a time to meet.

Chapter 30

Taking Responsibility

By Howard and William Hendricks

*Heaven's eternal wisdom has decreed that
man should ever stand in need of man.*

THEOCRITUS

When our family was quite young, we had a little ritual that our kids begged us to repeat as often as possible. We would line them up in the hallway, and one by one have them stand with their backs to the back of a closet door. Using a ruler on top of their heads, we would mark a line on the door and write the date and their heights. In this way we developed a simple growth chart. The kids begged us to measure their growth.

One time when I was leaving town on a trip, Bev, my second daughter, told me that while I was gone, she was determined to grow. (We had just recently charted her height.)

Sure enough, when I arrived back in Dallas and stepped off the plane, Bev ran to greet me with the exciting news.

"Daddy! Daddy! Come home quick! You gotta see how much I growed!"

As soon as I arrived home, we got out a ruler and went to the growth chart to measure her progress. The distance between the new line and the most recent one couldn't have been more than a millimeter or two, but she jumped up and down, shouting, "See, Daddy! See, I told you! I did grow!"

Later that day, she and I got to talking in the living room. She asked me one of those questions that you wish kids wouldn't ask: "Daddy, why do big people stop growing?"

I don't know what I told her, but I'm sure it was very superficial. Probably something like, "Well, Bev, they don't exactly stop. They stop growing up, but then they start growing out!"

Anyway, long after she was grown and on her own, God was working me over with that question. Why do big people stop growing? And is there any way to get them started again?

THE PROCESS OF GROWTH

The Bible tells us that the goal of life in Christ is that we become like Christ. Jesus told His disciples that "everyone who is fully trained will be like his teacher" (Luke 6:40, NIV). In other words, by following Christ, we will eventually become like Christ.

Likewise, Paul said that we have been predestined to be conformed to the likeness of Jesus (Romans 8:29). In fact, the purpose of the church is to help us in "attaining to the whole measure of the fullness of Christ" (Ephesians 4:13, NIV). So Christlikeness is our ultimate objective.

But please note: Christlikeness involves more than just "spiritual" categories; it includes everything in our lives. Jesus is Lord of all (Colossians 1:15, 17). Therefore, He wants us to become like Him in all areas of our lives: the intellectual, the physical, the social, and the emotional, as well as the spiritual. Is that your goal—Christlikeness in every area?

Even Jesus "grew," we are told, in four areas: in "wisdom," the intellectual component; in "stature," the physical component; in "favor with God," the spiritual component; and in "favor with men," the social and emotional component (Luke 2:52, NIV). By growing in these various ways, He demonstrated that life is developmental. We are meant to mature, to increase our God-given capacities—all of them, not just the spiritual ones.

This principle was brilliantly illustrated in the life of one of my dear friends, who passed away not long ago at the age of eighty-six. The last time I saw her was when she came up to me at a Christmas party and said, "Well, Hendricks, I haven't seen you for a long time. What are the five best books you've read recently?"

Needless to say, she had a way of keeping you on your toes! Her attitude was, "Let's not sit here and bore each other. Let's get into a discussion. And if we can't find anything to discuss, let's get into an argument!"

She died in her sleep at her daughter's home in Dallas. When I went over to meet the family, her daughter told me that the night before, this woman had sat down at her desk and written out her goals for the next ten years.

I love it! This woman realized that life is all about growing. In fact, the minute you stop growing, you start dying. She never stopped growing. The only thing that stopped her was when her body finally gave out.

Peter's final charge to his readers was, "Grow in the grace and knowledge of our Lord and Savior Jesus Christ" (2 Peter

3:18, NIV). So the question becomes, Are you committed to change and growth?

MENTORING—A FORGOTTEN ART

In the days when the church was just getting started and the New Testament was being written, boys were groomed into men through the relationships they had with older men. Call it mentoring, apprenticing, tutoring, whatever—the lessons of life were learned through life-on-life relationships. In fact, this seems to be the pattern for personal development throughout Scripture.

These mentoring relationships were carried on not only by people of faith, but also by society in general. The method continued until about a hundred years ago, when the Industrial Revolution and other factors brought about a radical change in the way knowledge and skills are taught.

Nowadays, teaching means telling, and testing boils down to the student cramming as much information as possible into his head, and then regurgitating it onto a piece of paper during an exam.

I'll never forget the student I ran into at the seminary who was on his way to take a test. I started to engage him in conversation, but he said, "Don't touch me, Prof! I'll leak everything I know!"

That's not education. Yet how often we equate Bible knowledge with spirituality!

Back when I was in Wheaton College, I worked as a youth director in a church. We had a boy in the junior department who had memorized six hundred verses word-perfectly! Todd (not his real name) was amazing. You could give him any reference, and he had the verse down cold.

One day I was told that someone had been stealing

money out of the junior department offering. So I appointed myself as a committee of one to investigate, and—you guessed it—our six-hundred-verse prodigy turned out to be the culprit. I caught him red-handed.

So I took Todd into my office and confronted him with his wrongdoing. I even gave him a verse of Scripture to drive home my point—to which he proceeded to tell me that I had misquoted the verse.

Finally I said, "Do you see any connection between that verse of Scripture and your stealing from the offering?"

"No," Todd replied. "Well, maybe."

"What do you think is the connection?"

"I got caught."

This kid typified our flawed system of spiritual education. We tend to think that if someone has mastered the Bible, he's practically a spiritual giant. But from God's perspective, the name of the game is not knowledge—it's active obedience. It's not how much truth is in your head that counts, but how much is in your life. Hebrews 5:13–14 distinguishes between infants, who are not acquainted with the teaching about righteousness, and the mature, "who by constant use [or practice] have trained themselves to distinguish between good and evil" (NIV).

God is not impressed with how much I know (intellectually) of His Word; He wants to know how much like Christ I am becoming. In the spiritual realm, the opposite of ignorance is not knowledge; it's obedience. In fact, according to the New Testament's understanding of the term, to "know" and not to do is not to "know" at all.

And this is where mentoring could save the day. It becomes ever clearer to me that we really don't need more books, tapes, broadcasts, sermons, and the like to "teach" us how to live the Christian life. What we need are relationships with people who know Christ (experientially) and can help us know Him at our point of need. It's not enough to harangue someone with the exhortation to "follow Christ." We need mentors who can say, as Paul said, "Follow me, as I follow Christ"—models who flesh out what life in Christ is all about.

YOUR RESPONSIBILITY

So does this place all of the burden on mentors, to take us from one stage of growth to the next? By no means. It places a burden on you and me to go out and find people who can help us get to the next level.

The ball is in your court. Let me close with four things you can do to meet the challenge.

1. *Find a mentor.* Again, every man needs a Paul and a Barnabas, an older man and a peer. Don't get hung up with the age factor. Just look for men who you feel can help you grow and realize your life goals.

Finding mentors will take time and energy on your part, and you may have to wait a while for the right person to come along. But the effort to find that person will be worth it in terms of the growth you will experience.

2. *Make mentoring a way of life.* We're not talking about finding one single mentor for the rest of your life. That would be highly unusual. Even if you found such a long-term relationship, you would still need several mentors throughout the course of your life. You need a variety of perspectives, and different men will contribute different things at different stages of your development. Therefore, you always need to be on the lookout for godly mentors. It should become a way of life.

Of course, you should keep in mind that mentors are by

no means the only resource by which God intends to bring you to maturity. God always uses a constellation of factors to work in your life.

3. *Find mentors for your kids.* You can do an invaluable service to your children by keeping an eye out for potential mentors for them. Obviously, as a parent you play the primary role in the development of your kids. But you can't provide everything. God never intended that you should.

So you're wise to look for teachers, coaches, youth leaders, other parents, and people in the workplace who are willing to take your son or daughter under their wing. That way, your children won't have to grow up and say what perhaps you've been saying: "No one ever built into my life."

4. *Mentor someone else.* In addition to a Paul and Barnabas, every man needs a Timothy—a younger man into whose life he is building. Whatever God has given you, you have an obligation to share that with someone who needs it.

You Can Make a Difference

If you stop and think about it, it really takes very little to make a substantial difference in someone's life. Just consider the people who have been significant in your life. Did it require them to have remarkable skill or knowledge? Sometimes, maybe. But more often than not, what mattered was that they were there, that they cared, and that they communicated that they cared.

Can you do that? Can you give someone an hour of your time? Can you tell him stories from your own life about situations you've faced? Can you encourage him to hang in there when things are tough, and stand by him as he fights his battles? Can you pray with him and for him?

The process is not that complicated.

STUDY QUESTIONS

1. Read 1 John 2:12–14. These three verses indicate three categories of believers: children, young men, and fathers. How important is it in Scripture that you grow to be a "father" spiritually?

2. Can you think of anyone in your life right now that you could approach about being your mentor?

3. Do you know anyone who needs a mentor? Would you be willing to take the job?

Taken from *As Iron Sharpens Iron,* by Howard and William Hendricks. Copyright © 1995 by Howard G. Hendricks and William D. Hendricks. Published by Moody Press. Used by permission.

A Prayer for Protection Against Temptation

BY MARTIN LUTHER

We have three temptations or adversaries: the flesh, the world, and the devil. Therefore, we pray:

Dear Father, grant us grace that we may have control over the lust of the flesh. Help us to resist its desire to eat, to drink, to sleep overmuch, to be idle, to be slothful. Help us by fasting, by moderation in food and dress and sleep and work, by watching and labor, to bring the flesh into subjection and fit it for good works.

Help us to fasten its evil, unchaste inclinations and all its desires and incitements with Christ upon the cross, and to slay them, so that we may not consent to any of its allurements, nor follow after them. Help us when we see a beautiful person, or image or any other creature, that it may not be a temptation, but an occasion for love of chastity and for praising Thee in Thy creatures. When we hear sweet sounds and feel things that please the senses, help us to seek therein not lust, but Thy praise and honor.

Preserve us from the great vice of avarice and the desire for the riches of this world. Keep us, that we may not seek this world's honor and power, nor consent to the desire for them. Preserve us, that the world's deceit, presences, and false promises may not move us to walk in its ways.

Preserve us, that the wickedness and the adversities of the world may not lead us to impatience, revenge, wrath, or other vices. Help us to renounce the world's lies and deceits, its promises, and unfaithfulness, and all its good and evil (as we have already promised in baptism to do), to abide firmly in this renunciation, and to grow therein from day to day.

Preserve us from the suggestions of the devil, that we may not consent to pride, become self-satisfied, and despise others for the sake of riches, rank, power, knowledge, beauty, or other good gifts of Thine. Preserve us, that we fall not into hatred or envy for any cause. Preserve us, that we yield not to despair, that great temptation of our faith, neither now nor at our last hour.

Have in Thy keeping, heavenly Father, all who strive and labor against these great and manifold temptations. Strengthen those who are yet standing; raise up all those who have fallen and are overcome; and to all of us grant Thy grace, that in this miserable and uncertain life, incessantly surrounded by so many enemies, we may fight with constancy, and with a firm and knightly faith, and win the everlasting crown.

STUDY QUESTIONS

1. Take some time to pray this prayer. Read it slowly, and after each complete thought, stop and apply it to your own life. Write down any specifics if you need to.

2. If you're working through this book with a small group, use one of your sessions to pray for each member of the group and encourage them to follow the steps of this book to achieve personal victory through holiness.

"A Prayer for Protection Against Temptation," by Martin Luther. Public domain. Taken from *The Works of Martin Luther, Volume 2*. Baker Book House.

Multnomah Publishers®

The publisher and author would love to hear your comments about this book. *Please contact us at:*
www.breakthroughseries.com